The Siva Samhita

The Siva Samhita

Translated into English By
Rai Bahadur Srisa Chandra Vasu

GYAN

Published by

Gyan Publishing House
5, Ansari Road
Daryaganj, New Delhi-110002
Phone: 011-47034999, 9811692060
E-mail: books@gyanbooks.com

Distribution Network
gyanbooks.com
India, USA, Canada, UK, Australia, France

ISBN : 978-81-212-2374-4 (PB)

2nd Impression 2021

Printed at: Gyan Press, Delhi.

The Siva Samhita
Translated by: Rai Bahadur Srisa Chandra Vasu

TABLE OF CONTENTS.

SIVA SAMHITA.

CHAPTER I.

Existence one only.

एकं ज्ञानं नित्यमाद्यन्तशून्यं नान्यत् किञ्चिद्वर्त्तते वस्तु सत्यम् ।
यद्भेदोऽस्मिन्निन्द्रियोपाधिना वै ज्ञानस्यायं भासते नान्यथैव ॥ १ ॥

The Jñâna [Gnosis] alone is eternal; it is without beginning or end; there exists no other real substance. Diversities which we see in the world are results of sense-conditions; when the latter cease, then this Jñâna alone, and nothing else, remains.

अथ भक्तानुरक्तोऽहं वक्ति योगानुशासनम् ।
ईश्वरः सर्वभूतानामात्ममुक्तिप्रदायकः ॥ २ ॥
त्यक्त्वा विवादशीलानां मतं दुर्ज्ञानहेतुकम् ।
आत्मज्ञानाय भूतानामनन्यगतिचेतसाम् ॥ ३ ॥

2-3. I, Ishvara, the lover of my devotees, and Giver of spiritual emancipation to all creatures, thus declare the science of *Yoganusâsana* (the exposition of Yoga). In it are discarded all those doctrines of disputants, which lead to false knowledge. It is for the spiritual disenthralment of persons whose minds are undistracted and fully turned towards Me.

Differences of opinion.

सत्यं केचित्प्रशंसन्ति तपः शौचं तथापरे ।
क्षमां केचित्प्रशंसंति तथैव सममार्ज्जवम् ॥ ४ ॥

4. Some praise truth, others purification and asceticism; some praise forgiveness, others equality and sincerity.

केचिद्दानं प्रशंसन्ति पितृकर्म तथापरे ।
केचित्कर्म प्रशंसन्ति केचिद्वैराग्यमुत्तमम् ॥ ५ ॥

5. Some praise alms-giving, others laud sacrifices made in honor of one's ancestors; some praise action (*Karma*), others think dispassion (*Vairâgya*) to be the best.

केचिद्गृहस्थकर्माणि प्रशंसन्ति विचक्षणाः ।
अग्निहोत्रादिकं कर्म तथा केचित्परं विदुः ॥ ६ ॥

6. Some wise persons praise the performance of the duties of the householder ; other authorities hold up fire-sacrifice &c., as the highest.

मन्त्रयोगं प्रशंसन्ति केचित्तीर्थानुसेवनम् ।
एवं बहूनुपायांस्तु प्रवदन्ति हि मुक्तये ॥ ७ ॥

7. Some praise *Mantra Yoga*, others the frequenting of places of pilgrimage. Thus diverse are the ways which people declare for emancipation.

एवं व्यवसिता लोके कृत्याकृत्यविदो जनाः ।
व्यामोहमेव गच्छंति विमुक्ताः पापकर्मभिः ॥ ८ ॥

8. Being thus diversely engaged in this world, even those who still know what actions are good and what evil, though free from sin, become subject to bewilderment.

एतन्मतावलम्बी यो लब्ध्वा दुरितपुण्यके ।
भ्रमतीत्यवशः सोऽत्र जन्ममृत्युपरम्पराम् ॥ ९ ॥

9. Persons who follow these doctrines, having committed good and bad actions, constantly wander in the worlds, in the cycle of births and deaths, bound by dire necessity.

अन्यैर्मतिमतां श्रेष्ठैर्गुप्तालोकनतत्परैः ।
आत्मानो बहवः प्रोक्ता नित्याः सर्वगतास्तथा ॥ १० ॥

10. Others, wiser among the many, and eagerly devoted to the investigation of the occult, declare that the souls are many and eternal, and omnipresent.

यद्यत्प्रत्यक्षविषयं तदन्यन्नास्ति चक्षते ।
कुतः स्वर्गादयः सन्तीत्यन्ये निश्चितमानसाः ॥ ११ ॥

11. Others say,—" Only those things can be said to exist which are perceived through the senses and nothing besides them ; where is heaven or hell?" Such is their firm belief.

ज्ञानप्रवाह इत्यन्ये शून्यं केचित्परं विदुः ।
द्वावेव तत्त्वं मन्यन्तेऽपरे प्रकृतिपूरुषौ ॥ १२ ॥

12. Others believe the world to be a current of consciousness and no material entity ; some call the void as the greatest. Others believe in two essences—Matter (*Prakriti*) and Spirit (*Puruṣa*).

अत्यन्तभिन्नमतयः परमार्थपराङ्मुखाः ।
एवमन्ये तु संचिन्त्य यथामति यथाश्रुतम् ॥ १३ ॥
निरीश्वरमिदं प्राहुः सेश्वरञ्च तथापरे ।
वदन्ति विविधैर्भेदैः सुयुक्तया स्थितिकातराः ॥ १४ ॥

13-14. Thus believing in widely different doctrines, with faces turned away from the supreme goal, they think, according to their understanding and education, that this universe is without God; others believe there is a God, basing their assertions on various irrefutable arguments, founded on texts, declaring difference between soul and God, and anxious to establish the existence of God.

एते चान्ये च मुनयः संज्ञाभेदा पृथग्विधाः ।
शास्त्रेषु कथिता ह्येते लोकव्यामोहकारकाः ॥ १५ ॥
एतद्विवादशीलानां मतं वक्तुं न शक्यते ।
भ्रमन्त्यस्मिञ्जनाः सर्वे मुक्तिमार्गबहिष्कृताः ॥ १६ ॥

15-16. These and many other sages with various different denominations, have been declared in the *Śâstras* as leaders of the human mind into delusion. It is not possible to describe fully the doctrines of these persons so fond of quarrel and contention; people thus wander in this universe, being driven away from the path of emancipation.

Yoga the only true method.

आलोक्य सर्वशास्त्राणि विचार्य च पुनः पुनः ।
इदमेकं सुनिष्पन्नं योगशास्त्रं परं मतम् ॥ १७ ॥

17. Having studied all the *Sâstras* and having pondered over them well, again and again, this *Yoga Śâstra* has been found to be the only true and firm doctrine.

यस्मिन् याते सर्वमिदं यातं भवति निश्चितम् ।
तस्मिन्परिश्रमः कार्यः किमन्यच्छास्त्रभाषितम् ॥ १८ ॥

18. Since by *Yoga* all this verily is known as a certainty, all exertion should be made to acquire it. What is the necessity then of any other doctrines?

योगशास्त्रमिदं गोप्यमस्माभिः परिभाषितम् ।
सुभक्ताय प्रदातव्यं त्रैलोक्ये च महात्मने ॥ १९ ॥

19. This *Yoga Śâstra*, now being declared by us, is a very secret doctrine, only to be revealed to a high-souled pious devotee throughout the three worlds.

Karma Kâṇḍa.

कर्मकाण्डं ज्ञानकाण्डमिति वेदो द्विधा मतः ॥ २० ॥
भवति द्विविधो भेदो ज्ञानकाण्डस्य कर्मणः ॥ २० ॥

20. There are two systems (as found in the Vedâs). *Karma Kâṇḍa* (ritualism) and *Jñâna Kâṇḍa* (wisdom). *Jñâna Kâṇḍa* and *Karma Kâṇḍa* are again each subdivided into two parts.

द्विविधः कर्मकाण्डः स्यान्निषेधविधिपूर्वकः ॥ २१ ॥

21. The *Karma Kâṇḍa* is twofold—consisting of injunctions and prohibitions.

निषिद्धकर्मकरणे पापं भवति निश्चितम् ।
विधिना कर्मकरणे पुण्यं भवति निश्चितम् ॥ २२ ॥

22. Prohibited acts when done, will certainly bring forth sin; from performance of enjoined acts there certainly results merit.

त्रिविधो विधिकूटः स्यान्नित्यनैमित्तकाम्यतः ।
नित्येऽकृते किल्बिषं स्यात्काम्ये नैमित्तिके फलम् ॥ २३ ॥

23. The injunctions are threefold—*nitya* (regular), *naimittika* (occasional), and *kâmya* (optional). By the non-performance of *nitya* or daily rites there accrues sin; but by their performance no merit is gained. On the other hand, the occasional and optional duties, if done or left undone, produce merit or demerit.

द्विविधन्तु फलं ज्ञेयं स्वर्गो नरक एव च ।
स्वर्गो नानाविधश्चैव नरकोपि तथा भवेत् ॥ २४ ॥

24. Fruits of actions are twofold—heaven or hell. The heavens are of various kinds and so also hells are diverse.

पुण्यकर्माणि वै स्वर्गो नरकः पापकर्माणि ।
कर्मबंधमयी सृष्टिर्नान्यथा भवति ध्रुवम् ॥ २५ ॥

25. The good actions are verily heaven, and sinful deeds are verily hell; the creation is the natural outcome of *Karma* and nothing else.

जन्तुभिश्चानुभूयंते स्वर्गे नानासुखानि च ।
नानाविधानि दुःखानि नरके दुःसहानि वै ॥ २६ ॥

26. Creatures enjoy many pleasures in heaven; many intolerable pains are suffered in hell.

पापकर्मवशाद्दुःखं पुण्यकर्मवशात्सुखम् ।
तस्मात्सुखार्थी विविधं पुण्यं प्रकुरुते ध्रुवम् ॥ २७ ॥

27. From sinful acts pain, from good acts happiness, results. For the sake of happiness, men constantly perform good actions.

पापभेागावसाने तु पुनर्जन्म भवेत्खलु ।
पुण्यभेागावसाने तु नान्यथा भवति ध्रुवम् ॥ २८ ॥

28. When the sufferings for evil actions are gone through, then there take place re-births certainly; when the fruits of good actions have been exhausted, then also, verily, the result is the same.

स्वर्गेऽपि दुःखसंभेागः परश्रीदर्शनादिषु ।
ततेा दुःखमिदं सर्वं भवेन्नास्त्यत्र संशयः ॥ २९ ॥

29. Even in heaven there is experiencing of pain by seeing the higher enjoyment of others; verily, there is no doubt of it that this whole universe is full of sorrow.

तत्कर्मकल्पकैः प्रोक्तं पुण्यं पापमिति द्विधा ।
पुण्यपापमयेा बन्धो देहिनां भवति क्रमात् ॥ ३० ॥

30. The classifiers of *Karma* have divided it into two parts; good and bad actions; they are the veritable bondage of the embodied souls each in its turn.

इहामुत्र फलद्वेषी सफलं कर्म संत्यजेत् ।
नित्यनैमित्तिकं संङ्गं त्यक्त्वा येागे प्रवर्तते ॥ ३१ ॥

31. Those who are not desirous of enjoying the fruits of their actions in this or next world, should renounce all actions which are done with an eye to their fruits, and having similarly discarded the attachment for the daily and the *naimittika* acts, should employ themselves in the practice of Yoga.

Jñâna Kâṇḍa.

कर्मकाण्डस्य माहात्म्यं ज्ञात्वा येागी त्यजेत्सुधीः ।
पुण्यपापद्वयं त्यक्त्वा ज्ञानकाण्डे प्रवर्तते ॥ ३२ ॥

32. The wise Yogi, having realised the truth of *Karma Kâṇḍa* (works), should renounce them; and having left both virtue and vice, he must engage in *Jñâna Kâṇḍa* (knowledge).

आत्मा वाऽरेतु द्रष्टव्यः श्रोतव्येत्यादि यच्छ्रुतिः ॥
सा सेव्या तत्प्रयत्नेन मुक्तिदा हेतुदायिनी ॥ ३३ ॥

33. The Vedic texts,—"The spirit ought to be seen,"—"About it one must hear," &c., are the real saviours and givers of true knowledge. They must be studied with great care.

दुरितेषु च पुण्येषु येा धीवृत्तिं प्रचेादयात् ।
सेाऽहं प्रवर्तते मत्तो जगत्सर्वं चराचरम् ॥
सर्वं च दृश्यते मत्तः सर्वं च मयि लीयते ।
न तद्भिन्नोऽहमस्मीह मद्भिन्नो न तु किंचन ॥ ३४ ॥

34. That Intelligence, which incites the functions into the paths of virtue or vice, am I. All this universe, moveable and immoveable, is from me; all things are preserved by me; all are absorbed into me (at the time of *pralaya*); because there exists nothing but spirit and I am that spirit.—There exists nothing else.

जलपूर्णेष्वसंख्येषु शरावेषु यथा भवेत् ।
एकस्य भात्यसंख्यत्वं तद्भेदोऽत्र न दृश्यते ॥
उपाधिषु शरावेषु या संख्या वर्तते परा ।
सा संख्या भवति यथा रवौ चात्मनि तत्तथा ॥ ३५ ॥

35. As in innumerable cups full of water, many reflections of the sun are seen, but the substance is the same; similarly individuals, like cups, are innumerable, but the vivifying spirit, like the sun, is one.

यथैकः कल्पकः स्वप्ने नानाविधितयेष्यते ।
जागरेपि तथाप्येकस्तथैव बहुधा जगत् ॥ ३६ ॥

36. As in a dream the one soul creates many objects by mere willing; but on awaking everything vanishes but the one soul; so is this universe.

सर्पबुद्धिर्यथा रज्जौ शुक्तौ वा रजतभ्रमः ।
तद्वदेवमिदं विश्वं विवृतं परमात्मनि ॥ ३७ ॥

37. As through illusion a rope appears like a snake, or pearl-shell like silver; similarly, all this universe is superimposed in the *Paramâtmâ* (the Universal Spirit.)

रज्जुज्ञानाद्यथा सर्पो मिथ्यारूपो निवर्तते ।
आत्मज्ञानात्तथा याति मिथ्याभूतमिदं जगत् ॥ ३८ ॥

38. As, when the knowledge of the rope is obtained, the erroneous notion of its being a snake does not remain; so, by the arising of the knowledge of self, vanishes this universe based on illusion.

रौप्यभ्रान्तिरियं याति शुक्तिज्ञानाद्यथा खलु ॥ ४० ॥
जगद्भ्रान्तिरियं याति चात्मज्ञानात् सदा तथा ॥ ३९ ॥

39. As, when the knowledge of the mother-of-pearl is obtained, the erroneons notion of its being silver does not remain; so, through the knowledge of spirit, the world always appears a delusion.

यथा वंशे रगभ्रान्तिर्भवेद्भेकवसाञ्जनात् ।
तथा जगदिदं भ्रांतिरभ्यासकल्पनाञ्जनात् ॥ ४० ॥

40. As, when a man besmears his eyelids with the collyrium prepared from the fat of frogs, a bamboo appears like a serpent, so the world appears in the *Paramâtmâ*, owing to the delusive pigment of habit and imagination.

आत्मज्ञानाद्यथा नास्ति रज्जुज्ञानाद्भुजङ्गमः ।
यथा दोषवशाच्छुक्लः पीतो भवति नान्यथा ।
अज्ञानदोषादात्मापि जगद्भवति दुस्त्यजम् ॥ ४१ ॥

41. As through knowledge of rope the serpent appears a delusion; similarly, through spiritual knowledge, the world. As through jaundiced eyes white appears yellow; similarly, through the disease of ignorance, this world appears in the spirit;—an error very difficult to be removed.

दोषनाशे यथा शुक्लो गृह्यते रोगिणा स्वयम् ।
शुक्लज्ञानात्तथाऽज्ञाननाशादात्मा तथा कृतः ॥ ४२ ॥

42. As when the jaundice is removed the patient sees the colour as it is, so when delusive ignorance is destroyed, the true nature of the spirit is made manifest.

कालत्रयेपि न यथा रज्जुः सर्पो भवेदिति ।
तथात्मा न भवेद्विश्वं गुणातीतो निरञ्जनः ॥ ४३ ॥

43. As a rope can never become a snake, in the past, present or future; so the spirit which is beyond all *gunás* and which is pure, never becomes the universe.

आगमाऽपायिनोऽनित्यानाश्यत्वेनेश्वरादयः ।
आत्मबोधेन केनापि शास्त्रादेतद्विनिश्चितम् ॥ ४४ ॥

44. Some wise men, well-versed in Scriptures, receiving the knowledge of spirit, have declared that even Devas like Indra, etc., are non-eternal, subject to birth and death, and liable to destruction.

यथा वातवशात्सिन्धावुत्पन्नाः फेनबुद्बुदाः ।
तथात्मनि समुद्भूतं संसारं क्षणभंगुरम् ॥ ४५ ॥

45. Like a bubble in the sea rising through the agitation of the wind, this transitory world arises from the Spirit.

अभेदो भासते नित्यं वस्तुभेदो न भासते ।
द्विधात्रिधादिभेदोऽयं भ्रमत्वे पर्यवस्यति ॥ ४६ ॥

46. The Unity exists always; the Diversity does not exist always; there comes a time when it ceases: two-fold, three-fold, and manifold distinctions arise only through illusion.

यद्भूतं यच्च भाव्यं वै मूर्तामूर्तं तथैव च ।
सर्वमेव जगदिदं विवृतं परमात्मनि ॥ ४७ ॥

47. Whatever was, is or will be, either formed or formless, in short, all this universe is superimposed on the Supreme Spirit.

कल्पकैः कल्पिता विद्या मिथ्या जाता मृषात्मिका ।
एतन्मूलं जगदिदं कथं सत्यं भविष्यति ॥ ४८ ॥

48. Suggested by the Lords of suggestion comes out *Avidyâ.* It is born of untruth, and its very essence is unreal. How can this world with such antecedents (foundations) be true?

The Spirit.

चैतन्यात्सर्वमुत्पन्नं जगदेतच्चराचरम् ।
तस्मात्सर्वं परित्यज्य चैतन्यं तं समाश्रयेत् ॥ ४९ ॥

49. All this universe, moveable or immoveable, has come out of Intelligence. Renouncing everything else, take shelter in it (Intelligence.)

घटस्याभ्यंतरे बाह्ये यथाकाशं प्रवर्तते ।
तथात्माभ्यंतरे बाह्ये कार्यवर्गेषु नित्यशः ॥ ५० ॥

50. As space pervades a jar both in and out, similarly within and beyond this ever-changing universe, there exists one Universal Spirit.

असंलग्नं यथाकाशं मिथ्याभूतेषु पंचसु ।
असंलग्नस्तथात्मा तु कार्यवर्गेषु नान्यथा ॥ ५१ ॥

51. As the space pervading the five false states of matter does not mix with them, so the Spirit does not mix with this ever-changing universe.

ईश्वरादिजगत्सर्वमात्मव्याप्यं समन्ततः ।
एकोऽस्ति सच्चिदानंदः पूर्णो द्वैतविवर्जितः ॥ ५२ ॥

52. From Devas down to this material universe all are pervaded by one Spirit. There is one *Sachchidânanda* (Existence, Intelligence and Bliss) all-pervading and secondless.

यस्मात्प्रकाशको नास्ति स्वप्रकाशो भवेत्ततः ।
स्वप्रकाशो यतस्तस्मादात्मा ज्योतिः स्वरूपकः ॥ ५३ ॥

53. Since it is not illumined by another, therefore it is self-luminous; and for that self-luminosity, the very nature of Spirit is Light.

अवच्छिन्नो यतो नास्ति देशकालस्वरूपतः ।
आत्मनः सर्वथा तस्मादात्मा पूर्णो भवेत्खलु ॥ ५४ ॥

54. Since the Spirit in its nature is not limited by time, or space, it is therefore infinite, all-pervading and entirety itself.

यस्मान्न विद्यते नाशः पंचभूतैर्वृथात्मकैः ।
तस्मादात्मा भवेन्नित्यस्तन्नाशो न भवेत्खलु ॥ ५५ ॥

55. Since the Spirit is unlike this world, which is composed of five states of matter, that *are false* and subject to destruction, therefore, it is eternal. It is never destroyed.

यस्मात्तदन्यो नास्तीह तस्मादेकोऽस्ति सर्वदा ।
यस्मात्तदन्यो मिथ्या स्यादात्मा सत्यो भवेत् खलु ॥ ५६ ॥

56. Save and beyond it, there is no other substance, therefore, it is one; without it everything else is false; therefore, it is True Existence.

अविद्याभूतसंसारे दुःखनाशे सुखं यतः ।
ज्ञानादाद्यंतशून्यं स्यात्तस्मादात्मा भवेत्सुखम् ॥ ५७ ॥

57. Since in this world created by ignorance, the destruction of sorrow means the gaining of happiness; and, through Gnosis, immunity from all sorrow ensues; therefore, the Spirit is Bliss.

यस्मान्नाशितमज्ञानं ज्ञानेन विश्वकारणम् ।
तस्मादात्मा भवेज्ज्ञानं ज्ञानं तस्मात्सनातनम् ॥ ५८ ॥

58. Since by Gnosis is destroyed the Ignorance, which is the cause of the universe; therefore, the Spirit is Gnosis; and this Gnosis is consequently eternal.

कालतो विविधं विश्वं यदा चैव भवेदिदम् ॥
तदेकोऽस्ति स एवात्मा कल्पनापथवर्जितः ॥ ५९ ॥

59. Since in time this manifold universe takes its origin, therefore, there is One who is verily the Self, unchanging through all times. Who is one, and unthinkable.

बाह्यानि सर्वभूतानि विनाशं यान्ति कालतः ।
यतो वाचो निवर्त्तंते आत्मा द्वैतविवर्जितः ॥ ६० ॥

60. All these external substances will perish in the course of time; (but) that Spirit which is indescribable by word (will exist) without a second.

न खं वायुर्न चाग्निश्च न जलं पृथिवी न च ।
नैतत्कार्यं नेश्वरादि पूर्णैकात्मा भवेत्खलु ॥ ६१ ॥

61. Neither ether, air, fire, water, earth, nor their combinations, nor the Devas, are perfect; the Spirit alone is so.

Yoga and Mâyâ.

आत्मानमात्मनो योगी पश्यत्यात्मनि निश्चितम् ।
सर्वसंकल्पसंन्यासी त्यक्तमिथ्याभवग्रहः ॥ ६२ ॥

62. Having renounced all false desires and abandoned all false worldly chains, the Yogi sees certainly in his own spirit the Universal Spirit by the self.

आत्मानात्मनि चात्मानं दृष्ट्वानन्त' सुखात्मकम् ।
विस्मृत्य विश्व' रमते समाधेस्तीव्रतस्तथा ॥ ६३ ॥

63. Having seen the Spirit, that brings forth happiness, in his own spirit by the help of the self, he forgets this universe, and enjoys the ineffable bliss of *Samâdhi* (profound meditation.)

मायैव विश्वजननी नान्या तत्त्वधियापरा ।
यदा नाशं समायाति विश्व' नास्ति तदा खलु ॥ ६४ ॥

64. *Mâyâ* (illusion) is the mother of the universe. Not from any other principle has the universe been created; when this *Mâyâ* is destroyed, the world certainly does not exist.

हेय' सर्वमिदं यस्य मायाविलसितं यतः ।
ततो न प्रीतिविषयस्तनुवित्तसुखात्मकः ॥ ६५ ॥

65. He, to whom this world is but the pleasure-ground of *Mâyá*, therefore, contemptible and worthless, cannot find any happiness in riches, body, etc., nor in pleasures.

अरिर्मित्रमुदासीनस्त्रिविधं स्यादिदं जगत् ।
व्यवहारेषु नियतं दृश्यते नान्यथा पुनः ॥
प्रियाप्रियादिभेदस्तु वस्तुषु नियतः स्फुटम् ॥ ६६ ॥

66. This world appears in three different aspects to men—either friendly, inimical, or indifferent; such is always found in worldly dealings; there is distinction also in substances, as they are good, bad or indifferent.

आत्मोपाधिवशादेवं भवेत्पुत्रादि नान्यथा ।
मायाविलसितं विश्व' ज्ञात्वैवं श्रुतियुक्तितः ॥
अध्यारोपापवादाभ्यां लयं कुर्वन्ति योगिनः ॥ ६७ ॥

67. That one Spirit, through differentiation, verily becomes a son, a father, etc. The *Sacred Scriptures* have demonstrated the universe to be the freak of *Mâyá* (illusion). The Yogi destroys this phenomenal universe by realising that it is but the result of *Adhyâropa* (superimposition) and by means of *Apavâda* (refutation of a wrong belief).

Definition of a Parama Hansa.

निखिलोपाधिहीनो वै यदा भवति पूरुषः ।
तदा विवक्षतेऽखंडज्ञानरूपी निरंजनः ॥ ६८ ॥

68. When a person is free from the infinite distinctions and states of existence as caste, individuality etc., then he can say that he is *indivisible intelligence*, and *pure* Unit.

Emanation or Evolution.

सो कामयतः पुरुषः सृजते च प्रजाः स्वयम् ।
अविद्या भासते यस्मात्तस्मान्मिथ्या स्वभावतः ॥ ६९ ॥

69. The Lord willed to create his creatures; from His will came out *Avidyâ* (Ignorance), the mother of this false universe.

शुद्ध ब्रह्मत्व संबद्धो विद्यया सहितो भवेत् ।
ब्रह्मतेनसती याति यत आभासते नभः ॥ ७० ॥

70. There takes place the conjunction between the Pure Brahma and Avidyâ, from which arises Brahmâ, from which comes out the Âkâśa.

तस्मात्प्रकाशते वायुर्वायोरग्निस्ततो जलम् ।
प्रकाशते ततः पृथ्वी कल्पनेयं स्थिता सति ॥ ७१ ॥

71. From the Akâsa emanated the air; from air came the fire; from fire—water; and from water came the earth. This is the order of subtle emanation.

आकाशाद्वायुराकाशपवनादग्निसंभवः ।
खवाताग्नेर्जलं व्योमवाताग्निवारितो मही ॥ ७२ ॥

72. From ether, air; from the air and ether combined came fire; from the triple compound of ether, air and fire came water; and from the combination of ether, air, fire and water was produced the (gross) earth.

खं शब्दलक्षणं वायुश्चंचलः स्पर्शलक्षणः ।
स्याद्रूपलक्षणं तेजः सलिलं रसलक्षणम् ॥
गन्धलक्षणिका पृथ्वी नान्यथा भवति ध्रुवम् ॥ ७३ ॥

73. The quality of ether is sound; of air motion and touch. Form is the quality of fire, and taste of water. And smell is the quality of the earth. There is no gainsaying this.

स्यादेकगुणमाकाशं द्विगुणो वायुरुच्यते ।
तथैव त्रिगुणं तेजो भवन्त्यापश्चतुर्गुणाः ॥
शब्दः स्पर्शश्च रूपं च रसो गन्धस्तथैव च ।
एतत्पंचगुणा पृथ्वी कल्पकैः कल्प्यतेऽधुना ॥ ७४ ॥

74. Akâsa has one quality; air two, fire three, water four, and earth five qualities, *viz*,—sound, touch, taste, form and smell. This has been declared by the wise.

चक्षुषा गृह्यते रूपं गन्धो घ्राणेन गृह्यते ।
रसो रसनया स्पर्शस्त्वचा संगृह्यते परम् ॥ ७५ ॥
श्रोत्रेण गृह्यते शब्दो नियतं भाति नान्यथा ॥ ७६ ॥

75-76. Form is perceived through the eyes, smell through the nose, taste through the tongue, touch through the skin and sound through the ear. These are verily the organs of perception.

चैतन्यात्सर्वमुत्पन्नं जगदेतच्चराचरम् ।
अस्ति चेत्कल्पनेयं स्यान्नास्ति चेदस्ति चिन्मयम् ॥ ७७ ॥

77. From Intelligence has come out all this universe, movable and immovable; whether or not its existence can be inferred, the "All Intelligence" One does exist.

Absorption or Involution.

पृथ्वी शीर्णा जले मग्ना जलं मग्नञ्च तेजसि ।
लीनं वायौ तथा तेजो व्योम्नि वातो लयं ययौ ॥
अविद्यायां महाकाशो लीयते परमे पदे ॥ ७८ ॥

78. The earth becomes subtle and is dissolved in water; water is resolved into fire; fire similarly merges in air; air gets absorption in ether, and ether is resolved in *Avidyâ* (Ignorance), which merges into the Great Brahma.

विक्षेपावरणा शक्तिर्दुरन्तासुखरूपिणी ॥
जडरूपा महामाया रजःसत्त्वतमोगुणा ॥ ७९ ॥

79. There are two forces—*vikṣepa*, (the out-going energy) and *âvarana* (the transforming energy) which are of great potentiality and power, and whose form is happiness. The great *Mâyâ*, when non-intelligent and material, has three attributes *sattva* (rhythm) *rajas* (energy) and *tamas* (inertia).

सा मायावरणाशक्त्यावृताविज्ञानरूपिणी ॥
दर्शयेज्जगदाकारं तं विक्षेपस्वभावतः ॥ ८० ॥

80. The non-intelligent form of *Mâyâ* covered by the *âvarana* force (concealment), manifests itself as the universe, owing to the nature of *vikṣepa* force.

तमो गुणाधिका विद्या या सा दुर्गा भवेत् स्वयम्
ईश्वर स्तदुपहितं चैतन्यं तदभूद् ध्रुवम् ॥
सत्ताधिका च या विद्या लक्ष्मीः स्याद्दिव्यरूपिणी ।
चैतन्यं तदुपहितं विष्णुर्भवति नान्यथा ॥ ८१ ॥

81. When the *avidyâ* has an excess of *tamas*, then it manifests itself as Durga; the intelligence which presides over her is called Iśvara.

81 (a). When the *Avidyâ* has an excess of *Sattva*, it manifests itself as the beautiful Lakṣhmi; the Intelligence which presides over her is called Vishnu.

रजोगुणाधिका विद्या ज्ञेया सा वै सरस्वती ।
यश्चित्स्वरूपो भवति ब्रह्मा तदुपधारकः ॥ ८२ ॥

82. When the *avidyâ* has an excess of *rajas*, it manifests itself as the wise Saraswati; the intelligence which presides over her is known as Brahmâ.

ईशाद्याः सकला देवा दृश्यन्ते परमात्मनि ।
शरीरादिजडं सर्वं सा विद्या तत्तथा तथा ॥ ८३ ॥

83. Gods like Śiva, Brahmâ, Vishnu, etc., are all seen in the great Spirit; bodies and all material objects are the various products of *avidyâ*.

एवंरूपेण कल्पन्ते कल्पका विश्वसम्भवम् ॥
तत्त्वातत्त्वं भवंतीह कल्पनान्येन चोदिता ॥ ८४ ॥

84. The wise have thus explained the creation of the world—*tattwas* (elements) and *not-tattwas* (non-elements) are thus produced—not otherwise.

प्रमेयत्वादिरूपेण सर्वं वस्तु प्रकाश्यते ।
विशेषशब्दोपादाने भेदो भवति नान्यथा ॥ ८५ ॥

85. All things are seen as finite, etc. (endowed with qualities, etc.), and there arise various distinctions merely through words and names; but there is no real difference.

तथैव वस्तुनास्त्येव भासको वर्तकः परः ।
स्वरूपत्वेन रूपेण स्वरूपं वस्तु भाष्यते ॥ ८६ ॥

86. Therefore, the things do not exist; the great and glorious One that manifests them, alone exists; though things are false and unreal, yet, as the reflection of the real, they, for the time being, appear real.

एकः सत्तापूरितानन्दरूपः पूर्णो व्यापी वर्तते नास्ति किञ्चित् ।
एतज्ज्ञानं यः करोत्येव नित्यं मुक्तः स स्यान्मृत्युसंसारदुःखात् ॥८७॥

87. The One Entity, blissful, entire and all-pervading, alone exists, and nothing else; he who constantly realises this knowledge is freed from death and the sorrow of the world-wheel.

यस्यारोपापवादाभ्यां यत्र सर्वं लयं गताः ।
स एको वर्तते नान्यत्तच्चित्तेनावधार्यते ॥ ८८ ॥

88. When, through the knowledge that all is illusory perception (âropa) and by intellectual refutation (apavâda) of other doctrines, this universe is resolved into the one, then, there exists that One and nothing else; then this is clearly perceived by the mind.

Karma clothes the Jiva with body.

पितुरन्नमयात्कोशाज्जायते पूर्वकर्मणः ।
तच्छरीरं विदुर्दुःखं स्वप्राग्भोगाय सुन्दरम् ॥ ८९ ॥

89. From the *Annamaya Koṣa* (the physical vehicle) of the father, and in accordance with its past *karma*, the human soul is re-incarnated; therefore, the wise consider this beautiful body as a punishment, for the suffering of the effects of past Karma.

मांसास्थिस्नायुमज्जादिनिर्मितं भोगमन्दिरम् ।
केवलं दुःखभोगाय नाडी संततिगुल्फितम् ॥ ९० ॥

90. This temple of suffering and enjoyment (human body), mad up of flesh, bones, nerves, marrow, blood, and intersected with blood vessels etc., is only for the sake of suffering of sorrow.

पारमेष्ठ्यमिदं गात्रं पंचभूतविनिर्मितम् ।
ब्रह्माण्डसंज्ञकं दुःखसुखभोगाय कल्पितम् ॥ ९१ ॥

91. This body, the abode of Brahma, and composed of five elements and known as Brahmâṇḍa (the egg of Brahmâ or microcosm) has been made for the enjoyment of pleasure or suffering of pain.

बिन्दुः शिवो रजः शक्तिरुभयोर्मिलनात्स्वयम् ।
स्वप्नभूतानि जायन्ते स्वशक्त्या जडरूपया ॥ ९२ ॥

92. From the self-combination of the Spirit which is Śiva and the Matter which is Śakti, and, through their inherent inter-action on each other, all creatures are born.

तत्पञ्चीकरणात्स्थूलान्यसंख्यानि समासतः ।
ब्रह्माण्डस्थानि वस्तूनि यत्र जीवोऽस्ति कर्मभिः ॥
तद्भूतपञ्चकात्सर्वं भोगाय जीवसंज्ञिता ॥ ९३ ॥

93. From the fivefold combination of all subtle elements, in this universe, gross innumerable objects are produced. The intelligence that is confined in them, through Karma, is called the *Jîva*. All this world is derived from the five elements. The *Jîva* is the enjoyer of the fruits of action.

पूर्वकर्मानुरोधेन करोमि घटनामहम् ।
अजडः सर्वभूतस्थो जडस्थित्या भुनक्ति तान् ॥ ९४ ॥.

94. In conformity with the effects of the past *karma* of the *Jîvas*, I regulate all their destinies. *Jîva* is immaterial, and is in all things; but it enters the material body to enjoy the fruits of *karma*.

जडात्स्वकर्मभिर्बद्धो जीवाख्यो विविधो भवेत् ।
भोगायोत्पद्यते कर्म ब्रह्मांडाख्ये पुनः पुनः ॥ ९५ ॥

95. Bound in the chain of matter by their *karma*, the *Jîvas* receive various names. In this world, they come again and again to undergo the consequences of their *karma*.

जीवश्च लीयते भोगावसाने च स्वकर्मणः ॥ ९६ ॥

96. When the fruits of *karma* have been enjoyed, the *Jîva* is absorbed in the *Parambrahma*.

Chapter II.

(1). *The microcosm.*

देहेऽस्मिन्वर्तते मेरुः सप्तद्वीपसमन्वितः ।
सरितः सागराः शैलाः क्षेत्राणि क्षेत्रपालकाः ॥ १ ॥

In this body, the mount *Meru—i.e.*, the vertebral column—is surrounded by seven islands; there are rivers, seas, mountains, fields; and lords of the fields too.

ऋषयो मुनयः सर्वे नक्षत्राणि ग्रहास्तथा ।
पुण्यतीर्थानि पीठानि वर्तन्ते पीठदेवताः ॥ २ ॥

2. There are in it seers and sages; all the stars and planets as well. There are sacred pilgrimages, shrines; and presiding dieties of the shrines.

सृष्टिसंहारकर्तारौ भ्रमन्तौ शशिभास्करौ ।
नभो वायुश्च वन्हिश्च जलं पृथ्वी तथैव च ॥ ३ ॥

3. The sun and moon, agents of creation and destruction, also move in it. Ether, air, fire, water and earth are also there.

(2). *The Nerve Centres.*

त्रैलोक्ये यानि भूतानि तानि सर्वाणि देहतः ।
मेरुं संवेष्ट्य सर्वत्र व्यवहारः प्रवर्तते ॥ ४ ॥

4. All the beings that exist in the three worlds are also to be found in the body; surrounding the *Meru* they are engaged in their respective functions.

जानाति यः सर्वमिदं स योगी नात्र संशयः ॥ ५ ॥

5. (But ordinary men do not know it). He who knows all this is a Yogî; there is no doubt about it.

ब्रह्माण्डसंज्ञके देहे यथादेशं व्यवस्थितः ।
मेरुशृंगे सुधारश्मिर्बहिरष्टकलायुतः ॥ ६ ॥

6. In this body, which is called Brahmâṇḍa (microcosm, literally the mundane egg), there is the nectar-rayed moon, in its proper place, on the top of the spinal cord, with eight Kalâs (in the shape of a semi-circle).

वर्ततेऽहर्निशं सोऽपि सुधां वर्षत्यधोमुखः ।
ततोऽमृतं द्विधाभूतं याति सूक्ष्मं यथा च वै ॥ ७ ॥

7. This has its face *downwards*, and rains nectar day and night. The ambrosia further sub-divides itself into two subtle parts:

इडामार्गेण पुष्ट्यर्थं याति मन्दाकिनीजलम् ।
पुष्णाति सकलं देहमिडामार्गेण निश्चितम् ॥ ८॥

8. One of these, through the channel named Iḍâ, goes over the body *to nourish* it, like the waters of the heavenly Ganges—certainly this ambrosia nourishes the whole body through the channel of Iḍâ.

एष पीयूषरश्मिर्हि वामपार्श्वे व्यवस्थितः ॥
अपरः शुद्धदुग्धाभो हठात्कर्षति मण्डलात् ।
मध्यमार्गेण सृष्ट्यर्थं मेरौ संयाति चन्द्रमाः ॥ ९ ॥

9. This milk-ray (moon) is on the left side. The other ray, brilliant as the purest milk and fountain of great joy, enters through the middle path (called *Sushumnâ*) into the spinal cord, in order to *create* this moon.

मेरुमूले स्थितः सूर्यः कलाद्वादशसंयुतः ।
दक्षिणे पथि रश्मिभिर्वहत्यूर्ध्वं प्रजापतिः ॥ १॥ ॥

10 At the bottom of the *Meru* there is the sun having twelve Kalâs. In the right side path (Pingalâ) the lord of creatures carries (the fluid) through its rays *upwards*.

पीयूषरश्मिनिर्यासं धातूंश्च ग्रसति ध्रुवम् ।
समीरमण्डले सूर्यो भ्रमते सर्वविग्रहे ॥ ११ ॥

11. It certainly swallows the vital secretions, and ray-exuded nectar. Together with the atmosphere, the sun moves through the whole body.

एषा सूर्यपरामूर्तिः निर्वाणं दक्षिणे पथि ।
वहते लग्नयोगेन सृष्टिसंहारकारकः ॥ १२ ॥

12. The right-side vessel, which is *pingalâ* is another form of the sun, and is the giver of Nirvâna. The lord of creation and destruction (the sun) moves in this vessel through auspicious ecliptical signs.

(3).—*The Nerves.*

सार्धलक्षत्रयं नाड्यः सन्ति देहान्तरे नृणाम् ।
प्रधानभूता नाड्यस्तु तासु मुख्याश्चतुर्दश ॥ १३ ॥

13. In the body of man there are 3,50,000 *nâḍis*; of them, the principal are fourteen;

सुषुम्णेडा पिंगला च गांधारी हस्तिजिह्विका ।
कुहूः सरस्वती पूषा शंखिनी च पयस्विनी ॥ १४ ॥
वारुण्यलम्बुसा चैव विश्वोदरी यशस्विनी ।
एतासु तिस्रो मुख्याः स्युः पिङ्गलेडा सुषुम्णिका ॥ १५ ॥

14-15. Sushumṇâ, Iḍâ, Pingalâ, Gândhâri, Hastijihvikâ, Kuhu, Saraswati, Pusâ, Sankhini, Payaswani, Vâruni, Alumbusâ, Vishwodari, and Yaśaswani. Among these Iḍâ, Pingalâ and Sushumnâ are the chief.

3

तिसृष्वेका सुषुम्नैव मुख्या सायोगिवल्लभा ।
अन्यास्तदाश्रयं कृत्वा नाड्यः सन्ति हि देहिनाम् ॥ १६ ॥

16. Among these three, Sushumṇâ alone is the highest and beloved of the Yogis. Other vessels are subordinate to it in the body.

नाड्यस्तु ता अधोवक्त्राः पद्मतन्तुनिभाः स्थिताः ।
पृष्ठवंशं समाश्रित्य सोमसूर्याग्निरूपिणी ॥ १७ ॥

17. All these principal *nâḍis* (vessels) have their mouths downwards, and are like thin threads of lotus. They are all supported by the vertebral column, and represent the sun, moon and fire.

तासां मध्ये गता नाडी चित्रा सा मम वल्लभा ।
ब्रह्मरन्ध्रञ्च तत्रैव सूक्ष्मात्सूक्ष्मतरं शुभम् ॥ १८ ॥

18. The innermost of these three is *Chitrâ*; it is my beloved. In that there is the subtlest of all hollows called Brahmarandhra.

पञ्चवर्णोज्ज्वला शुद्धा सुषुम्ना मध्यचारिणी ।
देहस्योपाधिरूपा सा सुषुम्ना मध्यरूपिणी ॥ १९ ॥

19. Brilliant with five colours, pure, moving in the middle of Sushumṇâ, this Chitrâ is *the* vital part of body and centre of Sushumṇâ.

दिव्यमार्गमिदं प्रोक्तममृतानन्दकारकम् ।
ध्यानमात्रेण योगीन्द्रो दुरितौघं विनाशयेत् ॥ २० ॥

20. This has been called in the Śâstras the Heavenly Way; this is the giver of the joy of immortality; by contemplating it, the great Yogî destroys all sins.

(4).—*The Pelvic Region.*

गुदात्तु द्व्यङ्गुलादूर्ध्वं मेढ्रात्तु द्व्यङ्गुलादधः ।
चतुरङ्गुलविस्तारमाधारं वर्तते समम् ॥ २१ ॥

21. Two digits above the rectum and two digits below the organ is the *âdhâra* lotus, having a dimension of four digits.

तस्मिन्नाधारपद्मे च कर्णिकायां सुशोभना ।
त्रिकोणा वर्तते योनिः सर्वतंत्रेषु गोपिता ॥ २२ ॥

22. In the pericarp of the *âdhâra* lotus there is the triangular, beautiful *yoni*, hidden and kept secret in all the Tantras.

तत्र विद्युल्लताकारा कुण्डली परदेवता ।
सार्द्धत्रिकरा कुटिला सुषुम्ना मार्गसंस्थिता ॥ २३ ॥

23. In it is the supreme goddess *Kuṇḍalini* of the form of electricity, in a coil. It has three coils and a half (like a serpent), and is in the mouth of Sushumṇâ.

जगत्संसृष्टिरूपा सा निर्माणे सततोद्यता ।
वाचामवाच्या वाग्देवी सदा देवैर्नमस्कृता ॥ २४ ॥

24. It represents the creative force of the world, and is always engaged in creation. It is the goddess of speech, whom speech cannot manifest, and who is praised by all gods.

इडानाम्नी तु या नाडी वाममार्गे व्यवस्थिता ।
सुषुम्णायां समाश्लिष्य दक्षनासापुटे गता ॥ २५ ॥

25. The *nâḍi* called Iḍâ is on the left side coiling round the Sushumṇâ, it goes to the right nostril.

पिङ्गला नाम या नाडी दक्षमार्गे व्यवस्थिता ।
मध्यनाडीं समाश्लिष्य वामनासापुटे गता ॥ २६ ॥

26. The *nâḍi* called Pingalâ is on the right side; coiling round the central vessel, it enters the left nostril.

इडापिंगलयोर्मध्ये सुषुम्णा या भवेत्खलु ।
षट्स्थानेषु च षटशक्तिं षट्पद्मं योगिनो विदुः ॥ २७ ॥

27. The *nâḍi* which is between Idâ and Pingalâ is certainly Sushumṇâ. It has six stages, six forces,* six lotuses, known to the Yogis.

पंचस्थानं सुषुम्णाया नामानि स्युर्बहूनि च ।
प्रयोजनवशात्तानि ज्ञातव्यानीह शास्त्रतः ॥ २८ ॥

28. The first five stages † of Sushumṇâ are known under various names; being necessary, they have been made known in this book.

अन्या याऽस्त्यपरा नाडी मूलाधारात्समुत्थिता ।
रसनामेढ्रनयनं पादांगुष्ठे च श्रोत्रकम् ॥
कुक्षिकक्षांगुष्ठकर्णं सर्वांगं पायुकुक्षिकम् ।
लब्ध्वा तां वै निवर्तन्ते यथादेशसमुद्भवाः ॥ २९ ॥

29. The other *nâḍis*, rising from *Mulâdhâr*, go to the various parts of the body, *e.g.* the tongue, organ, eyes, feet, toes, ears, the abdomen, the armpit, fingers of the hands, the scrotum and the anus. Having risen from their proper place, they stop at their respective destinations, as above described.

एताभ्य एव नाडीभ्यः शाखोपशाखतः क्रमात् ।
सार्धलक्षत्रयं जातं यथाभागं व्यवस्थितम् ॥ ३० ॥

30. From all these (fourteen) *nâḍis*, there arise gradually other branches and sub-branches, so that at last they become three hundred thousand and a half in number, and supply their respective places.

* That is, the functions of the Cord, *viz*:—Reflection, co-ordination, etc.

† The parts of which the Spinal Cord is composed are the Tantrik stages *viz.*:—Cervical, Dorsal, Lumbar, Sacral and Coccygeal.

एता भोगवहा नाड्यो वायुसञ्चारदक्षकाः ।
ओतप्रोताः सुसंव्याप्य तिष्ठन्त्यस्मिन्कलेवरे ॥ ३१ ॥

31. These *nâḍis* are spread through the body cross-wise and lengthwise; they are vehicles of sensation and keep watch over the movements of the air *i.e.*, they regulate the motor functions also.

(5).—*The Abdominal Region.*

सूर्यमण्डलमध्यस्थः कलाद्वादशसंयुतः ।
वस्तिदेशे ज्वलद्वह्निर्वर्तते चान्नपाचकः ॥
एष वैश्वानरोऽग्निर्वै मम तेजोंशसम्भवः ।
करोति विविधं पाकं प्राणिनां देहमास्थितः ॥ ३२ ॥

32. In the abdomen there burns the fire—digestor of food—situated in the middle of the sphere of the sun having twelve Kalâs. Know this as the fire of Vaiswânara; it is born from a portion of my own energy, and digests the various foods of creatures, being inside their bodies.

आयुः प्रदायको वह्निर्बलं पुष्टिं ददाति सः ।
शरीरपाटवञ्चापि ध्वस्तरोगसमुद्भवः ॥ ३३ ॥

33. This fire increases life, and gives strength and nourishment, makes the body full of energy, destroys all diseases, and gives health.

तस्माद्वैश्वानराग्निञ्च प्रज्वाल्य विधिवत्सुधीः ।
तस्मिन्नन्नं हुनेद्योगी प्रत्यहं गुरुशिक्षया ॥ ३४ ॥

34. The wise Yogi, having kindled this Viswânaric fire according to proper rites, should sacrifice food into it every day, in conformity with the teachings of his spiritual teacher.

ब्रह्माण्डसंज्ञके देहे स्थानानि स्युर्बहूनि च ।
मयोक्तानि प्रधानानि ज्ञातव्यानीह शास्त्रके ॥ ३५ ॥

35. This body called the Brahmâṇḍa (microcosm) has many parts, but I have enumerated the most important of them in this book. (Surely) they ought to be known.

नानाप्रकारनामानि स्थानानि विविधानि च ।
वर्तन्ते विग्रहे तानि कथितुं नैव शक्यते ॥ ३६ ॥

36. Various are their names, and innumerable are the places in this human body; all of them cannot be enumerated here.

(16).—*The Jivâtmâ.*

इत्थं प्रकल्पिते देहे जीवो वसति सर्वगः ।
अनादिवासनामालाऽलंकृतः कर्मशृंखलः ॥ ३७ ॥

37. In the body thus described, there dwelleth the Jîva, all-pervading, adorned with the garland of endless desires and chained (to the body) by *karma*.

नानाविधगुणोपेतः सर्वव्यापारकारकः ।
पूर्वार्जितानि कर्माणि भुनक्ति विविधानि च ॥ ३८ ॥

38. The Jîva possessed of many qualities and the agent of all events, enjoys the fruit of his various *karmas* amassed in the past life.

यद्यत्संदृश्यते लोके सर्वं तत्कर्मसम्भवम् ।
सर्वो कर्मानुसारेण जन्तुर्भोगान्भुनक्ति वै ॥३९ ॥

39. Whatever is seen among men (whether pleasure or pain) is born of *karma*. All creatures enjoy or suffer, according to the results of their actions.

ये ये कामादयो दोषाः सुखदुःखप्रदायकाः ।
ते ते सर्वे प्रवर्तन्ते जीवकर्मानुसारतः ॥ ४० ॥

40. The desires, etc., which cause pleasure or pain, act according to the past *karma* of the Jîva.

पुण्योपरक्तचैतन्ये प्राणान्प्रीणाति केवलम् ।
बाह्ये पुण्यमयं प्राप्य भोज्यवस्तु स्वयम्भवेत् ॥ ४१ ॥

41. The Jîva that has accumulated an excess of good and virtuous actions receives a happy life; and in the world he gets pleasant and good things to enjoy, without any trouble.

ततः कर्मबलात्पुंसः सुखं वा दुःखमेव च ।
पापोपरक्तचैतन्यं नैव तिष्ठति निश्चितम् ॥
न तद्भिन्नो भवेत्सोऽपि तद्भिन्नो न तु किञ्चन ।
मायोपहितचैतन्यात्सर्वं वस्तु प्रजायते ॥ ४२ ॥

42. In proportion to the force of his *karma*, man suffers misery or enjoys pleasure. The Jîva that has accumulated an excess of evil never stays in peace—it is not separate from its *karmas*; except *karma*, there is nothing in this world. From the Intelligence veiled by *Mâyâ*, all things have been evolved.

यथाकालेपि भोगाय जन्तूनां विविधोद्भवः ।
यथा दोषवशाच्छुक्तौ रजतारोपणं भवेत् ॥
तथा स्वकर्मदोषाद्वै ब्रह्मण्यारोप्यते जगत् ॥ ४३ ॥

43. As in their proper season, various creatures are born to enjoy the consequences of their *karma*; as through mistake a pearl-shell is taken for silver, so through the taint of one's own *karmas*, a man mistakes Brahman for the material universe.

सवासनाभ्रमोत्पन्नोन्मूलनातिसमर्थनम् ।
उत्पन्नश्चेदीदृशं स्याज्ज्ञानं मोक्षप्रसाधनम् ॥ ४४ ॥

44. From desire all these delusions arise; they can be eradicated with great difficulty; when the salvation-giving knowledge of the unreality of the world arises, then are desires destroyed.

साक्षाद्वैशेषदृष्टिस्तु साक्षात्कारिणि विभ्रमे ।
कारणं नान्यथा युक्त्या सत्यं सत्यं मयोदितम् ॥ ४५ ॥

45. Being engrossed in the manifested (objective) world, the delusion arises about that which is the manifestor—the subject. There is no other, (cause of this delusion). Verily, verily, I tell you the truth.

साक्षात्कारिभ्रमे साक्षात्साक्षात्कारिणि नाशयेत् ।
सो हि नास्तीति संसारे भ्रमो नैव निवर्तते ॥ ४६ ॥

46. The illusion of the manifested (objective world) is destroyed when the Maker of the Manifest becomes manifest. This illusion does not cease so long as one thinks, "Brahm is not."

मिथ्याज्ञाननिवृत्तिस्तु विशेषदर्शनाद्भवेत् ।
अन्यथा न निवृत्तिः स्याद्दृश्यते रजतभ्रमः ॥ ४७ ॥

47. By looking closely and deeply into the matter, this false knowledge vanishes. It cannot be removed otherwise; the delusion of silver remains.

यावन्नोत्पद्यते ज्ञानं साक्षात्कारे निरञ्जने ।
तावत्सर्वाणि भूतानि दृश्यन्ते विविधानि च ॥ ४८ ॥

48. As long as knowledge does not arise about the stainless Manifestor of the universe, so long all things appear separate and many.

यदा कर्मार्जितं देहं निर्वाणे साधनं भवेत् ।
तदा शरीरवहनं सफलं स्यान्न चान्यथा ॥ ४९ ॥

49. When this body, obtained through *karma*, is made the means of obtaining Nirvâṇa (divine beatitude); then only the carrying of the burden of the body becomes fruitful,—not otherwise.

यादृशी वासना मूला वर्त्तते जीवसंगिनी ।
तादृशं वहते जन्तुः कृत्याकृत्यविधौ भ्रमम् ॥ ५० ॥

50. Of whatever nature is the original desire (vâsanâ), that clings to and accompanies the Jîva (through various incarnations); similar is the delusion which it suffers, according to its deeds and misdeeds.

संसारसागरं तर्तुं यदीच्छेद्योगसाधकः ।
कृत्वा वर्णाश्रमं कर्म फलवर्जं तदाचरेत् ॥ ५१ ॥

51. If the practiser of Yoga wishes to cross the ocean of the world, he should perform all the duties of his *âshrama*, (the condition of life), renouncing all the fruits of his works.

विषयासक्तपुरुषा विषयेषु सुखेप्सवः ।
वाचाभिरुद्धनिर्वाणा वर्तन्ते पापकर्मणि ॥ ५२ ॥

52. Persons attached to sensual objects and desirous of sensual pleasures, descend from the road of Nirvâṇa, through the delusion of much talk, and fall into sinful deeds.

आत्मानमात्मना पश्यन्न किञ्चिदिह पश्यति ।
तदा कर्मपरित्यागे न दोषोऽस्ति मतं मम ॥ ५३ ॥

53. When a person does not see anything else here, having seen the Self by the self; then there is no sin (for him if he) renounces all ritual works. This is my opinion.

कामादयो विलीयन्ते ज्ञानादेव न चान्यथा ।
अभावे सर्वतत्त्वानां स्वयं तत्त्वं प्रकाशते ॥ ५४ ॥

54. All desires and the rest are dissolved through Gnosis only, and not otherwise. When all (minor) tattvas (principles), cease to exist, then My Tattva becomes manifest.

CHAPTER III.

On Yoga Practice. The Vâyus.

हृद्यस्ति पङ्कजं दिव्यं दिव्यलिङ्गेन भूषितम् ।
कादिठान्ताक्षरोपेतं द्वादशार्णविभूषितम् ॥ १ ॥

In the heart, there is a brilliant lotus with twelve petals adorned with brilliant signs. It has the letters from k to th (*i.e.*, k, kh, g. gh, ṅ, ch, chh. j, jh, ñ, ṭ, ṭh.), the twelve beautiful letters.

प्राणो वसति तत्रैव वासनाभिरलंकृतः ।
अनादिकर्मसंश्लिष्टः प्राप्याहङ्कारसंयुतः ॥ २ ॥

2. The *Prâna* lives there, adorned with various desires, accompanied by its past works, that have no beginning, and joined with egoism (*ahankâra.*)

Note:—The heart is in the centre where there is the seed यं

प्राणस्य वृत्तिभेदेन नामानि विविधानि च ।
वर्तन्ते तानि सर्वाणि कथितुं नैव शक्यते ॥ ३ ॥

3. From the different modifications of the *Prâna*, it receives various names; all of them cannot be stated here.

प्राणोऽपानः समानश्चोदानो व्यानश्च पञ्चमः ।
नागः कूर्मश्च कृकरो देवदत्तो धनञ्जयः ॥ ४ ॥

4. *Prâna, apâna, samâna, udâna, vyâna, nâga, kurma, Kṛikara, devadatta,* and *dhananjaya.*

दश नामानि मुख्यानि मयोक्तानीह शास्त्रके ।
कुर्वन्ति तेऽत्र कार्याणि प्रेरितानि स्वकर्मभिः ॥ ५ ॥

5. These are the ten principal names, described by me in this Śâstra; they perform all the functions, incited thereto by their own actions.

अत्रापि वायवः पञ्च मुख्याः स्युर्दशतः पुनः ।
तत्रापि श्रेष्ठकर्त्तारौ प्राणापानौ मयोदितौ ॥ ६ ॥

6. Again, out of these ten, the first five are the leading ones; even among these, the *Prâna* and *Apâna* are the highest agents, in my opinion.

हृदि प्राणो गुदेऽपानः समानो नाभिमण्डले ।
उदानः कण्ठदेशस्थो व्यानः सर्वशरीरगः ॥ ७ ॥

7. The seat of the *Prâna* is the heart; of the *apâna*, anus; of the *samâna*, the region about the navel; of the *udâna*, the throat; while the *vyâna* moves all over the body.

नागादिवायवः पञ्च ते कुर्वन्ति च विग्रहे ।
उद्गारोन्मीलनं क्षुत्तृड्जृम्भा हिक्का च पञ्चमः ॥ ८ ॥

8. The five remaining *vâyus*, the *nâga*, etc., perform the following functions in the body :—Eructation, opening the eyes, hunger and thirst, gaping or yawning, and lastly hiccup.

अनेन विधिना यो वै ब्रह्माण्डं वेत्ति विग्रहम् ।
सर्वपापविनिर्मुक्तः स याति परमां गतिम् ॥ ९ ॥

9. He who in this way knows the microcosm of the body, being absolved from all sins, reaches the highest state.

(2).—*The Guru.*

अधुना कथयिष्यामि क्षिप्रं योगस्य सिद्धये ।
यज्ज्ञात्वा नावसीदन्ति योगिनो योगसाधने ॥ १० ॥

10. Now I shall tell you, how easily to attain success in Yoga, by knowing which the Yogis never fail in the practice of Yoga.

भवेद्वीर्यवती विद्या गुरुवक्त्रसमुद्भवा ।
अन्यथा फलहीना स्यान्निर्वीर्याप्यतिदुःखदा ॥ ११ ॥

11. Only the knowledge imparted by a Guru, through his lips, is powerful and useful; otherwise it becomes fruitless, weak and very painful.

गुरुं सन्तोष्य यत्नेन ये वै विद्यामुपासते ।
अवलम्बेन विद्यायास्तस्याः फलमवाप्नुयात् ॥ १२ ॥

12. He who is devoted to any knowledge, while pleasing his Guru with every attention, readily obtains the fruit of that knowledge.

गुरुः पिता गुरुर्माता गुरुर्देवो न संशयः ।
कर्मणा मनसा वाचा तस्मात्सर्वैः प्रसेव्यते ॥ १३ ॥

13. There is not the least doubt that Guru is father, Guru is mother, and Guru is God even; and as such, he should be served by all with their thought, word and deed.

गुरुप्रसादतः सर्वं लभ्यते शुभमात्मनः ।
तस्मात्सेव्यो गुरुर्नित्यमन्यथा न शुभं भवेत् ॥ १४ ॥

14. By Guru's favour everything good relating to one's self is obtained. So the Guru ought to be daily served; else there can be nothing auspicious.

प्रदक्षिणत्रयं कृत्वा स्पृष्ट्वा सव्येन पाणिना ।
अष्टांगेन नमस्कुर्याद् गुरुपादसरोरुहम् ॥ १५ ॥

15. Let him salute his Guru after walking three times round him, and touching with his right hand his lotus-feet.

(3).—*The Adhikâri.*

श्रद्धयात्मवतां पुंसां सिद्धिर्भवति निश्चिता ।
अन्येषाञ्च न सिद्धिः स्यात्तस्माद्यत्नेन साधयेत् ॥ १६ ॥

16. The person who has control over himself attains verily success through faith; none other can succeed. Therefore, with faith, the Yoga should be practised with care and perseverance.

न भवेत्संगयुक्तानां तथाऽविश्वासिनामपि ।
गुरुपूजाविहीनानां तथा च बहुसंगिनाम् ॥ १७ ॥
मिथ्यावादरतानां च तथा निष्ठुरभाषिणाम् ।
गुरुसन्तोषहीनानां न सिद्धिः स्यात्कदाचन ॥ १७ ॥

17. Those who are addicted to sensual pleasures or keep bad company, who are disbelievers, who are devoid of respect towards their Guru, who resort to promiscuous assemblies, who are addicted to false and vain controversies, who are cruel in their speech, and who do not give satisfaction to their Guru never attain success.

फलिष्यतीति विश्वासः सिद्धेः प्रथमलक्षणम् ।
द्वितीयं श्रद्धया युक्तं तृतीयं गुरुपूजनम् ॥
चतुर्थं समताभावं पञ्चमेन्द्रियनिग्रहम् ।
षष्ठं च प्रमिताहारं सप्तमं नैव विद्यते ॥ १८ ॥

18. The first condition of success is the firm belief that it (vidyâ) must succeed and be fruitful; the second condition is having faith in it; the third is respect towards the Guru; the fourth is the spirit of universal equality; the fifth is the restraint of the organs of sense; the sixth is moderate eating, these are all. There is no seventh condition.

योगोपदेशं संप्राप्य लब्ध्वा योगविदं गुरुम् ।
गुरूपदिष्टविधिना धिया निश्चित्य साधयेत् ॥ १९ ॥

19. Having received instructions in Yoga, and obtained a Guru who knows Yoga, let him practise with earnestness and faith, according to the method taught by the teacher.

(4).—*The Place, Etc.*

सुशोभने मठे योगी पद्मासनसमन्वितः ।
आसनोपरि संविश्य पवनाभ्यासमाचरेत् ॥ २० ॥

20. Let the Yogi go to a beautiful and pleasant place of retirement or a cell, assume the posture *padmâsana*, and sitting on a seat (made of *kusa* grass) begin to practise the regulation of breath.

समकायः प्राञ्जलिश्च प्रणम्य च गुरून् सुधीः ।
दक्षे वामे च विघ्नेशं क्षेत्रपालांबिकां पुनः ॥ २१ ॥

21. The wise beginner should keep his body firm and inflexible, his hands joined as if in supplication, and salute the Gurus on the left side. He should also pay salutations to Ganeśa on the right side, and again to the guardians of the worlds and goddess Ambikâ, who are on the left side.

(5).—*The Prâṇâyâma.*

ततश्च दक्षांगुष्ठेन निरुध्य पिंगलां सुधीः ।
इडया पूरयेद्वायुं यथाशक्त्या तु कुम्भयेत् ॥
ततस्त्यक्त्वा पिंगलयाशनैरेव न वेगतः ॥ २२ ॥

22. Then let the wise practitioner close with his right thumb the *pingalâ* (the right nostril), inspire air through the Iḍâ (the left nostril); and keep the air confined—suspend his breathing—as long as he can; and afterwards let him breathe out slowly, and not forcibly, through the right nostril.

पुनः पिंगलयाऽऽपूर्य यथाशक्त्या तु कुम्भयेत् ।
इडया रेचयेद्वायुं न वेगेन शनैःशनैः ॥ २३ ॥

23. Again, let him draw breath through the right nostril, and stop breathing as long as his strength permits; then let him expel the air through the left nostril, not forcibly, but slowly and gently.

इदं योगविधानेन कुर्याद्विंशतिकुम्भकान् ।
सर्वद्वन्द्वविनिर्मुक्तः प्रत्यहं विगतालसः ॥ २४ ॥

24. According to the above method of Yoga, let him practise twenty *kumbhakas* (stopping of the breath). He should practise this daily without neglect or idleness, and free from all duals (of love and hatred, and doubt and contention), etc.

प्रातःकाले च मध्याह्ने सूर्यास्ते चार्धरात्रके ।
कुर्यादेवं चतुर्वारं कालेष्वेतेषु कुम्भकान् ॥ २५ ॥

25. These *kumbhakas* should be practised four times:—once (1) *early* in the morning at sun-rise, (2) then at *mid-day*, (3) the third at *sun-set*, and (4) the fourth at mid-night.

इत्थं मासत्रयं कुर्यादनालस्यो दिने दिने ।
ततो नाडीविशुद्धिः स्यादविलम्बेन निश्चितम् ॥ २६ ॥

26. When this has been practised daily, for three months, with regularity, the *nâḍis* (the vessels) of the body will readily and surely be purified.

यदा तु नाडीशुद्धिः स्याद्योगिनस्तत्त्वदर्शिनः ।
तदा विध्वस्तदोषश्च भवेदारम्भसम्भवः ॥ २७ ॥

27. When thus the *nâḍis* of the truth-perceiving Yogi are purified, then his defects being all destroyed, he enters the first stage in the practice of Yoga called *âṛambha*.

चिह्नानि योगिनो देहे दृश्यन्ते नाडिशुद्धितः ।
कथ्यन्ते तु समस्तान्यङ्गानि संक्षेपतो मया ॥ २८ ॥

28. Certain signs are perceived in the body of the Yogi whose *nâḍis* have been purified. I shall describe, in brief, all these various signs.

समकायः सुगन्धिश्च सुकान्तिः स्वरसाधकः ।
आरम्भघटकश्चैव यथा परिचयस्तदा ॥
निष्पत्तिः सर्वयोगेषु योगावस्था भवन्ति ताः ॥ २९ ॥

29. The body of the person practising the regulation of breath becomes harmoniously developed, emits sweet scent, and looks beautiful and lovely. In all kinds of Yoga, there are four stages of *prâṇâyâma* :— 1, Ârambha-avasthâ (the state of beginning); 2, Ghaṭa-avasthâ (the state of co-operation of Self and Higher Self); 3, Parichaya-avasthâ (knowledge); 4, Nishpattiavasthâ (the final consummation).

आरम्भः कथितोऽस्माभिरधुना वायुसिद्धये ।
अपरः कथ्यते पश्चात्सर्वदुःखौघनाशनः ॥ ३० ॥

30. We have already described the beginning or Arambha-avasthâ of *prâṇâyâma*; the rest will be described hereafter. They destroy all sin and sorrow.

प्रौढवह्निः सुभोगी च सुखीसर्वाङ्गसुन्दरः ।
संपूर्णहृदयो योगी सर्वोत्साहबलान्वितः ॥
जायते योगिनोऽवश्यमेतत्सर्वं कलेवरे ॥ ३१ ॥

31. The following qualities are surely always found in the bodies of every Yogi :—Strong appetite, good digestion, cheerfulness, handsome figure, great courage, mighty enthusiasm and full strength.

अथ वर्ज्यं प्रवक्ष्यामि योगविघ्नकरं परम् ।
येन संसारदुःखाब्धिं तीर्त्वा यास्यन्ति योगिन ॥ ३२ ॥

32. Now I tell you the great obstacles to Yoga which must be avoided, as by their removal the Yogis cross easily this sea of worldly sorrow.

(6).—*The things to be renounced.*

आम्लं रूक्षं तथा तीक्ष्णं लवणं सार्षपं कटुम् ।
बहुलं भ्रमणं प्रातःस्नानं तैलविदाहकम् ॥

स्तेयं हिंसां जनद्वेषञ्चाहङ्कारमनार्जवम् ।
उपवासमसत्यञ्च मोक्षञ्च प्राणिपीडनम् ॥
स्त्रीसङ्गमग्निसेवां च बह्वालापं प्रियाप्रियम् ।
अतीव भोजनं योगी त्यजेदेतानि निश्चितम् ॥ ३३ ॥

33. The Yogi should renounce the following:—1 Acids, 2 astringents, 3 pungent substances, 4 salt, 5 mustard, and 6 bitter things; 7 much walking, 8 early bathing (before sunrise) and 9 things roasted in oil; 10 theft, 11 killing (of animals) 12 enmity towards any person, 13 pride, 14 duplicity, and 15 crookedness; 16 fasting, 17 untruth, 18 thoughts other than those of moksha, 19 cruelty towards animals; 20 companionship of women, 21 worship of (or handling or sitting near) fire, and 22 much talking, without regard to pleasantness or unpleasantness of speech, and lastly, 23 much eating.

(7).—*The means.*

उपायं च प्रवक्ष्यामि क्षिप्रं योगस्य सिद्धये ।
गोपनीयं साधकानां येन सिद्धिर्भवेत्खलु ॥ ३४ ॥

34. Now I will tell you the means by which success in Yoga is quickly obtained; it must be kept secret by the practitioner so that success may come with certainty.

घृतं क्षीरं च मिष्टान्नं ताम्बूलं चूर्णवर्जितम् ।
कर्पूरं निष्तुषं मिष्टं सुमठं सूक्ष्मरन्ध्रकम् ॥
सिद्धान्तश्रवणं नित्यं वैराग्यगृहसेवनम् ।
नामसङ्कीर्तनं विष्णोः सुनादश्रवणं परम् ॥
धृतिः क्षमा तपः शौचं ह्रीर्मतिर्गुरुसेवनम् ।
सदैतानि परं योगी नियमानि समाचरेत् ॥ ३५ ॥

35. The great Yogi should observe always the following observances:—He should use 1 clarified butter, 2 milk, 3 sweet food, and 4 betel without lime, 5 camphor; 6 kind words, 7 pleasant monastery or retired cell, having a small door; 8 hear discourses on truth, and 9 always discharge his household duties with *vairâgya* (without attachment) 10 sing the name of Vishnu; 11 and hear sweet music, 12 have patience, 13 constancy, 14 forgiveness, 15 austerities, 16 purifications, 17 modesty, 18 devotion, and 19 service of the Guru.

अनिलेऽर्कप्रवेशो च भोक्तव्यं योगिभिः सदा ।
वायौ प्रविष्टे शशिनि शयनं साधकोत्तमैः ॥ ३६ ॥

36 When the air enters the sun, it is the proper time for the Yogi to take his food (*i.e.*, when the breath flows through the *Pingalâ*); when

the air enters the moon, he should go to sleep (*i.e.*, when the breath flows through the left nostril or the *Iḍâ*).

सद्यो भुक्तेऽपि क्षुधिते नाभ्यासः क्रियते बुधैः ।
अभ्यासकाले प्रथमं कुर्यात्क्षीराज्यभोजनम् ॥ ३७ ॥

37. The Yoga (*prâṇâyâma*) should not be practised just after the meals, nor when one is very hungry; before beginning the practice, some milk and butter should be taken.

ततोऽभ्यासे स्थिरीभूते न तादृङ्नियमग्रहः ।
अभ्यासिना विभोक्तव्यं स्तोकं स्तोकमनेकधा ॥
पूर्वोक्तकाले कुर्यात्तु कुम्भकान्प्रतिवासरे ॥ ३८ ॥

38. When one is well established in his practice, then he need not observe these restrictions. The practitioner should eat in small quantities at a time, though frequently; and should practise *kumbhaka* daily at the stated times.

ततो यथेष्टा शक्तिः स्याद्योगिनो वायुधारणे ।
यथेष्टं धारणाद्वायोः कुम्भकः सिध्यति ध्रुवम् ॥
केवले कुम्भके सिद्धे किं न स्यादिह योगिनः ॥ ३९ ॥

39. When the Yogi can, of his will, regulate the air and stop the breath (whenever and how long) he likes, then certainly he gets success in *kumbhaka*, and from the success in *kumbhaka* only, what things cannot the Yogi command here?

The first stage.

स्वेदः संजायते देहे योगिनः प्रथमोद्यमे ।
यदा संजायते स्वेदो मर्दनं कारयेत्सुधीः ॥
अन्यथा विग्रहे धातुर्नष्टो भवति योगिनः ॥ ४० ॥

40. In the first stage of *prâṇâyâma*, the body of the Yogi begins to perspire. When it perspires, he should rub it well, otherwise the body of the Yogi loses its *dhâtu* (humors).

The second and third stages.

द्वितीये हि भवेत्कम्पो दार्दुरी मध्यमे मता ।
ततोऽधिकतराभ्यासाद्गगनेचरसाधकः ॥ ४१ ॥

41. In the second stage, there takes place the trembling of the body; in the third, the jumping about like a frog; and when the practice becomes greater, the adept walks in the air.

Vâyusiddhi.

योगी पद्मासनस्थोऽपि भुवमुत्सृज्य वर्तते ।
वायुसिद्धिस्तदा ज्ञेया संसारध्वान्तनाशिनी ॥ ४२ ॥

42. When the Yogi, though remaining in *Padmâsana*, can rise in the air and leave the ground, then know that he has gained *Vâyu-siddhi* (success over air), which destroys the darkness of the world.

तावत्कालं प्रकुर्वीत योगोक्तनियमग्रहम् ।
अल्पनिद्रा पुरीषं च स्तोकं मूत्रं च जायते ॥ ४३ ॥

43. But so long (as he does not gain it), let him practise observing all the rules and restrictions laid down above. From the perfection of *prâṇâyâma*, follows decrease of sleep, excrements and urine.

अरोगित्वमदीनत्वं योगिनस्तत्त्वदर्शिनः ।
स्वेदो लाला कृमिश्चैव सर्वथैव न जायते ॥ ४४ ॥

44. The truth-perceiving Yogi becomes free from disease, and sorrow or affliction ; he never gets (putrid) perspiration, saliva and intestinal worms.

कफपित्तानिलाश्चैव साधकस्य कलेवरे ।
तस्मिन्काले साधकस्य भोज्येष्वनियमग्रहः ॥ ४५ ॥

45. When in the body of the practitioner, there is neither any increase of phlegm, wind, nor bile ; then he may with impunity be irregular in his diet and the rest.

अत्यल्पं बहुधा भुक्त्वा योगी न व्यथते हि सः ।
अथाभ्यासवशाद्योगी भूचरीं सिद्धिमाप्नुयात् ॥
यथा दर्दुरजन्तूनां गतिः स्यात्पाणिताडनात् ॥ ४६ ॥

46. No injurious results then would follow, were the Yogi to take a large quantity of food, or very little, or no food at all. Through the strength of constant practice, the Yogi obtains *Bhuchari-siddhi*, he moves as the frog jumps over the ground, when frightened away by the clapping of hands.

सन्त्यत्र बहवो विघ्ना दारुणा दुर्निवारणाः ।
तथापि साधयेद्योगी प्राणैः कंठगतैरपि ॥ ४७ ॥

47. Verily, there are many hard and almost insurmountable obstacles in Yoga, yet the Yogi should go on with his practice at all hazards ; even were his life to come to the throat.

ततो रहस्युपाविष्टः साधकः संयतेन्द्रियः ।
प्रणवं प्रजपेद्दीर्घं विघ्नानां नाशहेतवे ॥ ४८ ॥

48. Then let the practitioner, sitting in a retired place and restraining his senses, utter by inaudible repetition, the long *pranava* OM, in order to destroy all obstacles.

Note.—The A.U.M. all three should be distinctly uttered.

पूर्वार्जितानि कर्माणि प्राणायामेन निश्चितम् ।
नाशयेत्साधको धीमानिहलोकोद्भवानि च ॥ ४९ ॥

49. The wise practitioner surely destroys all his *karma*, whether acquired in this life or in the past, through the regulation of breath.

पूर्वार्जितानि पापानि पुण्यानि विविधानि च ।
नाशयेत्षोडशप्राणायामेन योगि पुंगवः ॥ ५० ॥

50. The great Yogi destroys by sixteen *prâṇâyâmas* the various virtues and vices accumulated in his past life.

पापतूलचयानाहो प्रदहेत्प्रलयाग्निना ।
ततः पापविनिर्मुक्तः पश्चात्पुण्यानि नाशयेत् ॥ ५१ ॥

51. This *prâṇâyâma* destroys sin, as fire burns away a heap of cotton; it makes the Yogi free from sin; next it destroys the bonds of all his good actions.

प्राणायामेन योगीन्द्रो लब्ध्वैश्वर्याष्टकानि वै ।
पापपुण्योदधिं तीर्त्वा त्रैलोक्यचरतामियात् ॥ ५२ ॥

52. The mighty Yogi having attained, through *prâṇâyâma*, the eight sorts of psychic powers, and having crossed the ocean of virtue and vice, moves about freely through the three worlds.

Increase of duration.

ततोऽभ्यासक्रमेणैव घटिकात्रितयं भवेत् ।
येन स्यात्सकलासिद्धिर्योगिनः स्वेप्सिता ध्रुवम् ॥ ५३ ॥

53. Then gradually he should make himself able to practise for three *gharis* (one hour and a half at a time, he should be able to restrain breath for that period). Through this, the Yogi undoubtedly obtains all the longed-for powers.

Siddhis or Perfections.

वाक्सिद्धिः कामचारित्वं दूरदृष्टिस्तथैव च ।
दूरश्रुतिः सूक्ष्मदृष्टिः परकायप्रवेशनम् ॥
विण्मूत्रलेपने स्वर्णमदृश्यकरणं तथा ।
भवन्त्येतानि सर्वाणि खेचरत्वं च योगिनाम् ॥ ५४ ॥

54. The Yogi acquires the following powers:—*vâkya siddhi* (prophecy), transporting himself everywhere at will (*Kâmachâri*), clairvoyance (*duradristhi*), clairaudience (*durashruti*), subtle-sight (*shukshma-drishti*), and the power of entering another's body (*parakâypravesana*), turning base metals to gold by rubbing them with his excrements and urine, and the power of becoming invisible, and lastly, moving in the air.

II—The Ghata Avastha.

यदा भवेद्घटावस्था पवनाभ्यासने परा ।
तदा संसारचक्रेऽस्मिन्नास्ति यन्न सधारयेत् ॥ ५५ ॥

55. When, by the practice of *Prânâyâma*, the Yogi reaches the state of *ghata* (water-jar), then for him there is nothing in this circle of universe which he cannot accomplish.

प्राणापाननादबिंदुजीवात्मपरमात्मनः ।
मिलित्वा घटते यस्मात्तस्माद्वै घट उच्यते ॥ ५६ ॥

56. The *ghata* is said to be that state in which the *prâna* and the *apâna vâyus*, the *nâda* and the *vindu*, the *jivâtmâ* (the Human Spirit) and the *Paramâtmâ* (the Universal Spirit) combine and co-operate.

याममात्रं यदा धर्तुं समर्थः स्यात्तदाद्भुतः ।
प्रत्याहारस्तदैव स्यान्नांतरा भवति ध्रुवम् ॥ ५७ ॥

57. When he gets the power of holding breath (*i.e.*, to be in trance) for three hours, then certainly the wonderful state of *pratyâhâr* is reached without fail.

यं यं जानाति योगीन्द्रस्तं तमात्मेति भावयेत् ।
यैरिन्द्रियैर्यद्विधानस्तदिन्द्रियजयो भवेत् ॥ ५८ ॥

58. Whatever object the Yogi perceives, let him consider it to be the spirit. When the modes of action of various senses are known, then they can be conquered.

याममात्रं यदा पूर्णं भवेदभ्यासयोगतः ।
एकवारं प्रकुर्वीत तदा योगी च कुम्भकम् ॥
दण्डाष्टकं यदा वायुर्निश्चलो योगिनो भवेत् ।
स्वसामर्थ्यात्तदांगुष्ठे तिष्ठेद्वातुलवत्सुधीः ॥ ५९ ॥

59. When, through great practice, the Yogi can perform one *kumbhaka* for full three hours, when for eight *dandas* (=3 hours) the breathing of the Yogi is suspended, then that wise one can balance himself on his thumb; but he appears to others as insane.

III.—The Parichaya.

ततः परिचयावस्था योगिनोऽभ्यासतो भवेत् ।
यदा वायुश्चन्द्रसूर्यं त्यक्त्वा तिष्ठति निश्चलम् ॥
वायुः परिचितो वायुः सुषुम्ना व्योम्नि संचरेत् ॥ ६० ॥

60. After this, through exercise, the Yogi reaches the *Parichaya avasthâ*. When the air leaving the sun and the moon (the right and the left nostrils), remains unmoved and steady in the ether of the tube *sushumnâ*, then it is in the *parichaya* state.

क्रियाशक्तिं गृहीत्वैव चक्रान्भित्वा सुनिश्चितम् ।
यदा परिचयावस्था भवेदभ्यासयोगतः ॥
त्रिकूटं कर्मणां योगी तदा पश्यति निश्चितम् ॥ ६१ ॥

61. When he, by the practice of Yoga, acquires power of action (*kriyâ shakti*) and pierces through the six *chakras*, and reaches the sure condition of *parichaya*, then the Yogi, verily, sees the three-fold effects of *karma*.

ततश्च कर्मकूटानि प्रणवेन विनाशयेत् ।
स योगी कर्मभोगाय कायव्यूहं समाचरेत् ॥ ६२ ॥

62. Then, let the Yogi destroy the multitude of *karmas* by the *pranava* (OM); let him accomplish *kâyavyuha* (a mystical process of arranging the various *skandas* of the body), in order to enjoy or suffer the consequences of all his actions in one life, without the necessity of re-birth.

अस्मिन्काले महायोगी पंचधा धारणं चरेत् ॥
येन भूरादिसिद्धिः स्यात्ततो भूतभयापहा ॥ ६३ ॥

63. At that time let the great Yogi practise the five-fold *dhâranâ* forms of concentration on Vishnu, by which command over the five elements is obtained, and fear of injuries from any one of them is removed. (Earth, water, fire, air, *âkas* cannot harm him.)

Note.—He should perform 5 Kumbhakas at each centre or Chakra.

आधारे घटिकाः पंच लिंगस्थाने तथैव च ।
तदूर्ध्वं घटिकाः पञ्च नाभिहृन्मध्यके तथा ॥
भ्रूमध्योर्ध्वं तथा पंच घटिका धारयेत्सुधीः ।
तथा भूरादिना नष्टो योगीन्द्रो न भवेत्खलु ॥ ६४ ॥

64. Let the wise Yogi practise *dhâranâ* thus:—five *ghatis* (2½ hours) in the *âdhâra* lotus (Mulâdhara); five *ghatis* in the seat of the *linga* (Svâdhisthânâ), five *ghatis* in the region above it, (in the navel, Manipur), and the same in the heart (Anâhata); five *ghatis* in the throat (Visuddha) and, lastly let him hold *dhâranâ* for five *ghatis* in the space between the two eye-brows (Ajnâpur). By this practice the elements cease to cause any harm to the great Yogi.

मेधावी सर्वभूतानां धारणां यः समभ्यसेत् ।
शतब्रह्ममृतेनापि मृत्युस्तस्य न विद्यते ॥ ६५ ॥

65. The wise Yogi, who thus continually practises concentration (*dhâranâ*), never dies through hundreds of cycles of the great Brahmâ.

IV.—The Nishpatti.

ततोऽभ्यासक्रमेणैव निष्पत्तिर्योगिनो भवेत् ।
अनादिकर्मबीजानि येन तीर्त्वाऽमृतं पिबेत् ॥ ६६ ॥

66. After this, through gradual exercise, the Yogi reaches the *Nishpatti-avasthâ* (the condition of consummation). The Yogi, having destroyed all the seeds of *karma* which existed from the beginning, drinks the waters of immortality.

यदा निष्पत्तिर्भवति समाधेः स्वेनकर्मणा ।
जीवन्मुक्तस्य शांतस्य भवेद्धीरस्य योगिनः ॥
यदा निष्पत्तिसंपन्नः समाधिः स्वेच्छया भवेत् ।
गृहीत्वा चेतनां वायुः क्रियाशक्तिं च वेगवान् ॥
सर्वांश्चक्रान्विजित्वा च ज्ञानशक्तौ विलीयते ॥ ६७ ॥

67. When the *jivan-mukta* (delivered in the present life,) tranquil Yogi has obtained, through practice, the consummation of *samâdhi* (meditation), and when this state of consummated *samâdhi* can be voluntarily evoked, then let the Yogi take hold of the *chetanâ* (conscious intelligence), together with the air, and with the force of (*kriyâ-sakti*) conquer the six wheels, and absorb it in the force called *jñâna-sakti*.

इदानीं क्लेशहान्यर्थं वक्तव्यं वायुसाधनम् ।
येन संसारचक्रेऽस्मिन् भोगहानिर्भवेद्ध्रुवम् ॥ ६८ ॥

68. Now we have described the management of the air in order to remove the troubles (which await the Yogi); through this knowledge of *vâyu-sâdhanâ* vanish all sufferings and enjoyments in the circle of this universe.

रसनां तालुमूले यः स्थापयित्वा विचक्षणः ।
पिबेत्प्राणानिलं तस्य योगानां संक्षयो भवेत् ॥ ६९ ॥

69. When the skilful Yogi, by placing the tongue at the root of the palate, can drink the *prâṇa vâyu*, then there occurs complete dissolution of all Yogas (*i.e.*, he is no longer in need of Yoga).*

काकचंच्वा पिबेद्वायुं शीतलं यो विचक्षणः ।
प्राणापानविधानज्ञः स भवेन्मुक्तिभाजनः ॥ ७० ॥

70. When the skilful Yogi, knowing the laws of the action of *Prâṇa* and *Apâna*, can drink the cold air through the contraction of the mouth, in the form of a crow-bill, then he becomes entitled to liberation.

---

* Some texts read रोगाणां instead of योगानां in which case, it will mean "freedom from all diseases."

सरसं यः पिबेद्वायुं प्रत्यहं विधिना सुधीः ।
नश्यंति योगिनस्तस्य श्रमदाहजरामयाः ॥ ७१ ॥

71. That wise Yogi, who daily drinks the ambrosial air, according to proper rules, destroys fatigue, burning (fever), decay and old age, and injuries.

रसनामूर्ध्वगां कृत्वा यश्चन्द्रे सलिलं पिबेत् ।
मासमात्रेण योगीन्द्रो मृत्युं जयति निश्चितम् ॥ ७२ ॥

72. Pointing the tongue upwards, when the Yogi can drink the nectar flowing from the moon (situated between the two eye-brows), within a month he certainly would conquer death.

राजदंतबिलं गाढं संपीड्य विधिना पिबेत् ।
ध्यात्वा कुण्डलिनीं देवीं षण्मासेन कविर्भवेत् ॥ ७३ ॥

73. When having firmly closed the glottis by the proper yogic method, and contemplating on the goddess Kuṇḍalini, he drinks (the moon fluid of immortality), he becomes a sage or poet within six months.

काकचंच्वा पिबेद्वायुं सन्ध्ययोरुभयोरपि ।
कुण्डलिन्या मुखे ध्यात्वा क्षयरोगस्य शान्तये ॥ ७४ ॥

74. When he drinks the air through the crow-bill, both in the morning and the evening twilight, contemplating that it goes to the mouth of the Kuṇḍalini, consumption of the lungs (phthisis) is cured.

अहर्निशं पिबेद्योगी काकचंच्वा विचक्षणः ।
पिबेत्प्राणानिलं तस्य रोगाणां संक्षयो भवेत् ॥
दूरश्रुतिर्दूरदृष्टिस्तथा स्याद्दर्शनं खलु ॥ ७५ ॥

75. When the wise Yogi drinks the fluid day and night through the crow-beak, his diseases are destroyed: he acquires certainly the powers of clairaudience and clairvoyance.

दन्तैर्दन्तान्समापीड्य पिबेद्वायुं शनैः शनैः ।
ऊर्ध्वजिह्वः सुमेधावी मृत्युं जयति सोऽचिरात् ॥ ७६ ॥

76. When firmly closing the teeth (by pressing the upper on the lower jaw), and placing the tongue upwards, the wise Yogi drinks the fluid very slowly, within a short period he conquers death.

षण्मासमात्रमभ्यासं यः करोति दिने दिने ।
सर्वपापविनिर्मुक्तो रोगान्नाशयते हि सः ॥ ७७ ॥

77. One, who daily continues this exercise for six months only, is freed from all sins, and destroys all diseases.

संवत्सरकृताऽभ्यासाद्भैरवो भवति ध्रुवम् ।
अणिमादिगुणांल्लब्ध्वा जितभूतगणः स्वयम् ॥ ७८ ॥

78. If he continues this exercise for a year, he becomes a Bhairava; he obtains the powers of *aṇimâ* &c., and conquers all elements and the elementals.

रसनामूर्ध्वगां कृत्वा क्षणार्धं यदि तिष्ठति ।
क्षणेन मुच्यते योगी व्याधिमृत्युजरादिभिः ॥ ७९ ॥

79. If the Yogi can remain for half a second with his tongue drawn upwards, he becomes free from disease, death, and old age.

रसनां प्राणसंयुक्तां पीड्यमानां विचिंतयेत् ।
न तस्य जायते मृत्युः सत्यं सत्यं मयोदितम् ॥ ८० ॥

80. Verily, verily, I tell you the truth that the person never dies who contemplates by pressing the tongue, combined with the vital fluid or Prâṇa.

एवमभ्यासयोगेन कामदेवो द्वितीयकः ।
न क्षुधा न तृषा निद्रा नैव मूर्च्छा प्रजायते ॥ ८१ ॥

81. Through this exercise and Yoga, he becomes like a Kâmadeva, without a rival. He feels neither hunger, nor thirst, nor sleep, nor swoon.

अनेनैव विधानेन योगीन्द्रोऽवनिमण्डले ।
भवेत्स्वच्छन्दचारी च सर्वापत्परिवर्जितः ॥ ८२ ॥

82. Acting upon these methods the great Yogi becomes in the world perfectly independent; and freed from all obstacles, he can go everywhere.

न तस्य पुनरावृत्तिर्मोदते ससुरैरपि ।
पुण्यपापैर्न लिप्येत एतदाचरणेन सः ॥ ८३ ॥

83. By practising thus, he is never reborn, nor is tainted by virtue and vice, but enjoys (for ages) with the gods.

The postures.

चतुरशीत्यासनानि सन्ति नानाविधानि च ।
तेभ्यश्चतुष्कमादाय मयोक्तानि ब्रवीम्यहम् ॥
सिद्धासनं ततः पद्मासनञ्चोग्रं च स्वस्तिकम् ॥ ८४ ॥

84. There are eighty-four postures, of various modes. Out of them, four ought to be adopted, which I mention below:—1, Siddhâsana; 2, Padmâsana; 3, Ugrâsana; 4, Svastikâsana.

1.—*Siddhâsana.*

योनिं संपीड्य यत्नेन पादमूलेन साधकः ।
मेढोपरि पादमूलं विन्यसेद्योगवित्सदा ॥
ऊर्ध्वं निरीक्ष्य भ्रूमध्यं निश्चलः संयतेन्द्रियः ।
विशेषोऽवक्रकायश्च रहस्युद्वेगवर्जितः ॥
एतत्सिद्धासनं ज्ञेयं सिद्धानां सिद्धिदायकम् ॥ ८५ ॥

85. The Siddhâsana that gives success to the practitioner is as follows:—Pressing with care by the heel the *yoni*, the other heel the Yogi should place on the *lingam*; he should fix his gaze upwards on the space between the two eyebrows, should be steady, and restrain his senses. His body particularly must be straight and without any bend. The place should be a retired one, without any noise.

येनाभ्यासवशाच्छीघ्रं योगनिष्पत्तिमाप्नुयात् ।
सिद्धासनं सदा सेव्यं पवनाभ्यासिना परम् ॥ ८६ ॥

86. He who wishes to attain quick consummation of Yoga, by exercise, should adopt the Siddhâsana posture, and practise regulation of the breath.

येन संसारमुत्सृज्य लभते परमां गतिम् ।
नातः परतरं गुह्यमासनं विद्यते भुवि ॥
येनानुध्यानमात्रेण योगी पापाद्विमुच्यते ॥ ८७ ॥

87. Through this posture the Yogi, leaving the world, attains the highest end and throughout the world there is no posture more secret than this. By assuming and contemplating in this posture, the Yogi is freed from sin.

2.—*The Padmâsana.*

उत्तानौ चरणौ कृत्वा ऊरुसंस्थौ प्रयत्नतः ।
ऊरुमध्ये तथोत्तानौ पाणी कृत्वा तु तादृशौ ॥
नासाग्रे विन्यसेद्दृष्टिं दन्तमूलञ्च जिह्वया ।
उत्तोल्य चिबुकं वक्ष उत्थाप्य पवनं शनैः ॥
यथाशक्त्या समाकृष्य पूरयेदुदरं शनैः ।
यथा शक्त्यैव पश्चात्तु रेचयेदविरोधतः ॥
इदं पद्मासनं प्रोक्तं सर्वव्याधिविनाशनम् ॥ ८८ ॥

88. I describe now the Padmâsana which wards off (or cures) all diseases:—Having crossed the legs, carefully place the feet on the opposite thighs (*i.e.*, the left foot on the right thigh, and *vice versa*); cross both the hands and place them similarly on the thighs; fix the sight on the

tip of the nose; pressing the tongue against the root of the teeth, (the chin should be elevated, the chest expanded) then draw the air slowly, fill the chest with all your might, and expel it slowly, in an unobstructed stream.

दुर्लभं येन केनापि धीमता लभ्यते परम् ॥ ८९ ॥

89. It cannot be practised by everybody; only the wise attains success in it.

अनुष्ठाने कृते प्राणः समश्चलति तत्क्षणात् ।
भवेदभ्यासने सम्यक्साधकस्य न संशयः ॥ ९० ॥

90. By performing and practising this posture, undoubtedly the vital airs of the practitioner at once become completely equable, and flow harmoniously through the body.

पद्मासने स्थितो योगी प्राणापानविधानतः ।
पूरयेत्स विमुक्तः स्यात्सत्यं सत्यं वदाम्यहम् ॥ ९१ ॥

91. Sitting in the Padmâsana posture, and knowing the action of the *Práṇa* and *Apána*, when the Yogi performs the regulation of the breath, he is emancipated. I tell you the truth. Verily, I tell you the truth.

3.—*The Ugrâsana.*

प्रसार्य चरणद्वन्द्वं परस्परमसंयुतम् ।
स्वपाणिभ्यां दृढं धृत्वा जानूपरि शिरो न्यसेत् ॥
आसनोग्रमिदं प्रोक्तं भवेदनिलदीपनम् ।
देहावसानहरणं पश्चिमोत्तानसंज्ञकम् ॥
य एतदासनं श्रेष्ठं प्रत्यहं साधयेत्सुधीः ।
वायुः पश्चिममार्गेण तस्य सञ्चरति ध्रुवम् ॥ ९२ ॥

92. Stretch out both the legs and keep them apart; firmly take hold of head by the hands, and place them on the knees. This is called Ugrâsana (the stern-posture), it excites the motion of the air, destroys the dullness and uneasiness of the body, and is also called *Paschima-uttána* (the posterior crossed posture.) That wise man who daily practises this noble posture can certainly induce the flow of the air *per viam posteriori.*

एतदभ्यासशीलानां सर्वसिद्धिः प्रजायते ।
तस्माद्योगी प्रयत्नेन साधयेत्सिद्धमात्मनः ॥ ९३ ॥

93. Those who practise this obtain all the *siddhis*; therefore, those, desirous of attaining powers, should practise this diligently.

गोपनीयं प्रयत्नेन न देयं यस्य कस्यचित् ।
येन शीघ्रं मरुत्सिद्धिर्भवेद् दुःखौघनाशिनी ॥ ९४ ॥

94. This should be kept secret with the greatest care, and not be given to anybody and everybody. Through it, *váyu-siddhi* is easily obtained, and it destroys a multitude of miseries.

4.—*The svastikâsana.*

जानूर्वोरन्तरे सम्यग्धृत्वा पादतले उभे ।
समकायः सुखासीनः स्वस्तिकं तत्प्रचक्षते ॥ ९५ ॥

95. Place the soles of the feet completely under the thighs, keep the body straight, and sit at ease. This is called the Svastikâsana.

अनेन विधिना योगी मारुतं साधयेत्सुधीः ।
देहे न क्रमते व्याधिस्तस्य वायुश्च सिद्ध्यति ॥ ९६ ॥

96. In this way, the wise Yogi should practise the regulation of the air. No disease can attack his body, and he obtains *váyu siddhi.*

सुखासनमिदं प्रोक्तं सर्वदुःखप्रणाशनम् ।
स्वस्तिकं योगिभिर्गोप्यं स्वस्तीकरणमुत्तमम् ॥ ९७ ॥

97. This is also called the Sukhâsana, the easy posture. This health-giving, good Svastikâsana should be kept secret by the Yogi.

CHAPTER IV.

Yoni-Mudrâ. The Sacred Drink of the Kaulas.

आदौ पूरक योगेन स्वाधारे पूरयेन्मनः ।
गुदमेढ्रान्तरे योनिस्तामाकुञ्च्य प्रवर्तते ॥ १ ॥

First with a strong inspiration fix the mind in the *âdhâr* lotus. Then engage in contracting the Yoni, which is situated in the perineal space.

ब्रह्मयोनिगतं ध्यात्वा कामं कन्दुकसन्निभम् ।
सूर्यकोटि प्रतीकाशं चन्द्रकोटिसुशीतलम् ॥
तस्योर्ध्वं तु शिखासूक्ष्मा चिद्रूपा परमाकला ।
तया सहितमात्मानमेकीभूतं विचिन्तयेत् ॥ २ ॥

2 There let him contemplate that the God of Love resides in that Brahma Yoni and that he is beautiful like Bandhuk flower (*Pentapetes Phœnicia*)—brilliant as tens of millions of suns, and cool as tens of millions of moons. Above this (Yoni) is a very small and subtle flame, whose form is intelligence. Then let him imagine that a union takes place there between himself and that flame (the Śiva and Sakti).

गच्छति ब्रह्ममार्गेण लिंगत्रयक्रमेण वै ।
अमृतं तद्धि स्वर्गस्थं परमानन्दलक्षणम् ॥
श्वेतरक्तं तेजसाढ्यं सुधाधाराप्रवर्षिणम् ।
पीत्वा कुलामृतं दिव्यं पुनरेव विशेत्कुलम् ॥ ३ ॥

3. (Then imagine that)—There go up through the Sushumnâ vessel, the three bodies in their due order (*i.e.*, the etheric, the astral and the mental bodies). There is emitted in every chakra the nectar, the characteristic of which is great bliss. Its colour is whitish rosy (pink), full of splendour, showering down in jets the immortal fluid. Let him drink this wine of immortality which is divine, and then again enter the Kulâ (*i.e.*, perineal space.)

Note.—While these subtle bodies go up, they drink at every stage this nectar, called Kulâmrita.

पुनरेव कुलं गच्छेन्मात्रायोगेन नान्यथा ।
सा च प्राणसमाख्याता ह्यस्मिंस्तन्त्रे मयोदिता ॥ ४ ॥

4. Then let him go again to the Kulâ through the practice of *mâtrâ Yoga* (*i.e.*, prâṇâyâma.) This Yoni has been called by me in the Tantras as equal to life.

पुनः प्रलीयते तस्यां कालाग्न्यादिशिवात्मकम् ।
योनिमुद्रा परा ह्येषा बन्धस्तस्याः प्रकीर्तितः ।
तस्यास्तु बन्धमात्रेण तन्नास्ति यन्न साधयेत् ॥ ५ ॥

5. Again let him be absorbed in that Yoni, where dwells the fire of death—the nature of Shiva, &c. Thus has been described by me the method of practising the great Yoni-Mudrâ. From success in its practice, there is nothing which cannot be accomplished.

छिन्नरूपास्तु ये मन्त्राः कीलिताः स्तंभिताश्च ये ।
दग्धामन्त्राः शिखाहीना मलिनास्तु तिरस्कृताः ॥
मन्दा बालास्तथा वृद्धाः प्रौढा यौवनगर्विताः ।
अरिपक्षे स्थिता ये च निर्वीर्याः सत्त्ववर्जिताः ।
तथा सत्त्वेन हीनाश्च खण्डिताः शतधाकृताः ॥
विधानेन च संयुक्ताः प्रभवन्त्यचिरेण तु ।
सिद्धिमोक्षप्रदाः सर्वे गुरुणा विनियोजिताः ॥
दीक्षयित्वा विधानेन अभिषिच्य सहस्रधा ।
ततो मंत्राधिकारार्थमेषा मुद्रा प्रकीर्तिता ॥ ६ ॥

6. Even those mantras which are deformed (chhinna) or paralyzed (Kilita), scorched (stambhita) by fire, or whose flame has become attenuated, or which are dark, and ought to be abandoned, or which are evil, or too old, or which are proud of their budding youth, or have gone over to the side of the enemy, or weak and essenceless without vitality; or which have been divided into hundreds of parts, even they become fertile through time and method. All these can give powers and emancipation when properly given to the disciple by the Guru, after having initiated him according to proper rites, and bathed him a thousand times. This Yoni-mudrâ has been described. in order that the student may deserve (to be initiated into the mysteries of) and receive the mantras.

ब्रह्महत्यासहस्राणि त्रैलोक्यमपि घातयेत् ।
नासौ लिप्यति पापेन योनिमुद्रानिबन्धनात् ॥ ७ ॥

7. He who practises Yoni-Mudrá is not polluted by sin, were he to murder a thousand Brâhmanas or kill all the inhabitants of the three worlds:—

गुरुहा च सुरापी च स्तेयी च गुरुतल्पगः ।
एतैः पापैर्न बध्येत योनिमुद्रानिबन्धनात् ॥ ८ ॥

8. Were he to kill his teacher or drink wine or commit theft, or violate the bed of his preceptor, he is not stained by these sins also, by virtue of this mudrâ.

तस्मादभ्यसनं नित्यं कर्तव्यं मोक्षकांक्षिभिः ।
अभ्यासाज्जायते सिद्धिरभ्यासान्मोक्षमाप्नुयात् ॥ ९ ॥

9. Therefore, those who wish for emancipation should *practise* this daily. Through *practice* (*abhyâsa*), success is obtained; through practice one gains liberation.

संविदं लभतेऽभ्यासाद्योगोऽभ्यासात्प्रवर्तते ।
मुद्राणां सिद्धिरभ्यासादभ्यासाद्वायुसाधनम् ॥
कालवञ्चनमभ्यासात्तथा मृत्युञ्जयो भवेत् ॥ १० ॥

10. Perfect consciousness is gained through *practice*. Yoga is attained through *practice*; success in Mudrâs comes by *practice*; through *practice* is gained success in prâṇáyáma. Death can be cheated of its prey through *practice*, and man becomes the conqueror of death by *practice*.

वाक्सिद्धिः कामचारित्वं भवेदभ्यासयोगतः ॥
योनिमुद्रा परं गोप्या न देया यस्य कस्यचित् ।
सर्वथा नैव दातव्या प्राणैः कण्ठगतैरपि ॥ ११ ॥

11. Through *practice* one gets the power of *vâch* (prophecy), and the power of going everywhere, through mere exertion of will. This Yoni-mudrâ should be kept in great secrecy, and not be given to everybody. Even when threatened with death, it should not be revealed or given to others.

The Awakening of Kuṇḍalini.

अधुना कथयिष्यामि योगसिद्धिकरं परम् ।
गोपनीयं सुसिद्धानां योगं परमदुर्लभम् ॥ १२ ॥

12. Now I shall tell you the best means of attaining success in Yoga. The practitioners should keep it secret. It is the most inaccessible Yoga.

सुप्ता गुरुप्रसादेन यदा जागर्ति कुण्डली ।
तदा सर्वाणि पद्मानि भिद्यन्ते ग्रन्थयोऽपि च ॥ १३ ॥

13. When the sleeping goddess Kuṇḍalini is awakened, through the grace of Guru, then all the lotuses and the bonds are readily pierced through and through.

तस्मात्सर्वप्रयत्नेन प्रबोधयितुमीश्वरीम् ।
ब्रह्मरन्ध्रमुखे सुप्तां मुद्राभ्यासं समाचरेत् ॥ १४ ॥

14. Therefore, in order that the goddess, who is asleep in the mouth of the Brahmarandhra (the innermost hollow of Sushumnâ) be awakened, the Mudrâs should be practised with the greatest care.

महामुद्रा महाबन्धो महावेधश्च खेचरी ।
जालंधरो मूलबंधो विपरीतकृतिस्तथा ॥
उड्डानं चैव वज्रोणी दशमे शक्तिचालनम् ।
इदं हि मुद्रादशकं मुद्राणामुत्तमोत्तमम् ॥ १५ ॥

15. Out of the many Mudrâs, the following ten are the best :—(1) Mahâmudrâ, (2) Mahâbandha, (3) Mahâvedha, (4) Khechari, (5) Jâlandhar, (6) Mulabandha, (7) Viparítkaraṇa, (8) Uḍḍana, (9) Vajroṇdî, and (10) Shaktichâlana.

अथ महामुद्राकथनम् ।
महामुद्रां प्रवक्ष्यामि तन्त्रेऽस्मिन्मम वल्लभे ।
यां प्राप्य सिद्धाः सिद्धिं च कपिलाद्याः पुरागताः ॥ १६ ॥

16. My dearest, I shall now describe to you the Mahâmudrâ, from whose knowledge the ancient sages Kapila and others obtained success in Yoga.

(1.)—*Mahâ-Mudrâ.*

अपसव्येन संपीड्य पादमूलेन सादरम् ।
गुरूपदेशतो योनिं गुदमेढ्रान्तरालगाम् ॥
सव्यं प्रसारितं पादं धृत्वा पाणियुगेन वै ।
नवद्वाराणि संयम्य चिबुकं हृदयोपरि ॥
चित्तं चित्तपथे दत्त्वा प्रभवेद्वायुसाधनम् ।
महामुद्राभवेदेषा सर्वतन्त्रेषु गोपिता ॥
वामाङ्गेन समभ्यस्य दक्षाङ्गेनाभ्यसेत्पुनः
प्राणायामं समं कृत्वा योगी नियतमानसः ॥ १७ ॥

17. In accordance with the instructions of the Guru, press gently the perineum with the heel of the left foot. Stretching the right foot out, hold it fast by the two hands. Having closed the nine gates (of the body), place the chin on the chest. Then concentrate the vibrations of the mind and inspire air and retain it by kumbhaka (so long as one can comfortably keep it). This is the Mahâmudrâ, held secret in all the Tantras. The steady-minded Yogi, having practised it on the left side, should then practise it on the right side ; and in all cases must be firm in prâṇâyâma —the regulation of his breath.

अनेन विधिना योगी मन्दभाग्योपि सिध्यति ।
सर्वासामेव नाडीनां चालनं बिन्दुमारणम् ॥
जीवनन्तु कषायस्य पातकानां विनाशनम् ।
सर्वरोगोपशमनं जठराग्निविवर्धनम् ॥

वपुषा कान्तिममलां जरामृत्युविनाशनम्।
वांछितार्थफलं सौख्यमिन्द्रियाणाञ्च मारणम्॥
एतदुक्तानि सर्वाणि योगारूढस्य योगिनः।
भवेदभ्यासतोऽवश्यं नात्र कार्या विचारणा॥ १८॥

18. In this way, even the most unfortunate Yogi might obtain success. By this means all the vessels of the body are roused and stirred into activity; the life is increased and its decay is checked, and all sins are destroyed. All diseases are healed, and the gastric fire is increased. It gives faultless beauty to the body, and destroys decay and death. All fruits of desires and pleasures are obtained, and the senses are conquered. The Yogi fixed in meditation acquires all the above-mentioned things, through practice. There should be no hesitation in doing so.

गोपनीया प्रयत्नेन मुद्रेयं सुरपूजिते।
यां तु प्राप्य भवाम्भोधेः पारं गच्छन्ति योगिनः॥ १९॥

19. O ye worshipped of the gods! know that this Mudrâ is to be kept secret with the greatest care. Obtaining this, the Yogi crosses the ocean of the world.

मुद्रा कामदुघा ह्येषा साधकानां मयोदिता।
गुप्ताचारेण कर्तव्या न देया यस्य कस्यचित्॥ २०॥

20. This Mudrâ, described by me, is the giver of all desires to the practitioner; it should be practised in secrecy, and ought never to be given to everybody.

(2).—*Mahâ-Bandha.*

अथ महाबन्धकथनम्।

ततः प्रसारितः पादो विन्यस्य तमुरूपरि।
गुदयोनिं समाकुंच्य कृत्वा चापानमूर्ध्वगम्
योजयित्वा समानेन कृत्वा प्राणमधोमुखम्
बन्धयेदूर्ध्वगत्यर्थं प्राणापानेन यः सुधीः।
कथितोऽयं महाबन्धः सिद्धिमार्गप्रदायकः।
नाडीजालाद्रसव्यूहो मूर्धानं याति योगिनः।
उभाभ्यां साधयेत्पद्भ्यामेकैकं सुप्रयत्नतः॥ २१॥

21. Then (after Mâhamudrá), having extended the (right) foot, place it on the (left) thigh; contract the perineum, and draw the *apâna vâyû* upwards and join it with the *samâna vâyu*; bend the *prâna vâyû* downwards, and then let the wise Yogi bind them in trinity in the navel (*i.e.* the *prâna* and the *apâna* should be joined with the *Samâna* in the navel.)

I have told you now the Mahâbandha, which shows the way to emancipation. By this, all the fluids in the vessels of the body of the Yogi are propelled towards the head. This should be practised with great care, alternately with both feet.

भवेदभ्यासतो वायुः सुषुम्नां मध्यसङ्गतः ।
अनेन वपुषः पुष्टिर्दृढबन्धोऽस्थिपंजरे ॥
संपूर्णहृदयो योगी भवन्त्येतानि योगिनः ।
बन्धेनानेन योगीन्द्रः साधयेत्सर्वमीप्सितम् ॥ २२ ॥

22. Through this practice, the wind enters the middle channel of the Sushumnâ, the body is invigorated by it, the bones are firmly knitted, the heart of the Yogi becomes full (of cheerfulness) By this Bandha, the great Yogi accomplishes all his desires.

(3.) —*Mahâ-Vedha.*

अथ महावेधकथनम् ।
अपानप्राणयोरैक्यं कृत्वा त्रिभुवनेश्वरि ।
महावेधस्थितो योगी कुक्षिमापूर्य वायुना ।
स्फिचौ संताडयेद्धीमान्वेधोऽयं कीर्तितो मया ॥ २३ ॥

23. O goddess of the three worlds! when the Yogi, while performing the Mahâbandha, causes the union of the *prâna* and *apâna vâyus* and filling in the viscera with air drives it slowly towards the nates, it is called Mahâvedha.

वेधेनानेन संविध्य वायुना योगिपुंगवः ।
ग्रंथिं सुषुम्णामार्गेण ब्रह्मग्रंथिं भिनत्त्यसौ ॥ २४ ॥

24. The best of the Yogis having, through the help of the *vâyu*, pierced with this perforator the knot which is in the path of Sushumnâ, should then pierce the knot of Brahma.

यः करोति सदाभ्यासं महावेधं सुगोपितम् ।
वायुसिद्धिर्भवेत्तस्य जरामरणनाशिनी ॥ २५ ॥

25. He who practises this Mahâvedha with great secrecy, obtains *vâyu-siddhi* (success over the wind). It destroys decay and death.

चक्रमध्ये स्थिता देवाः कम्पन्ति वायुताडनात् ।
कुण्डल्यपि महामाया कैलासे सा विलीयते ॥ २६ ॥

26. The gods residing in the chakras tremble owing to the gentle influx and eflux of air in prâṇâyâma; the great goddess, Kuṇali Mahâ Mâyâ, is also absorbed in the mount Kailâsa.

महामुद्रामहाबन्धौ निष्फलौ वेधवर्जितौ ।
तस्माद्योगी प्रयत्नेन करोति त्रितयं क्रमात् ॥ २७ ॥

27. The Mahâmudra and Mahâbandha become fruitless if they are not followed by Mahâ-vedha; therefore, the Yogi should practise all these three successively with great care.

एतत्त्रयं प्रयत्नेन चतुर्वारं करोति यः ।
षण्मासाभ्यन्तरं मृत्युं जयत्येव न संशयः ॥ २८ ॥

28. He who practises these three daily four times with great care, undoubtedly conquers death within six months.

एतत्त्रयस्य माहात्म्यं सिद्धो जानाति नेतरः ।
यज्ज्ञात्वा साधकाः सर्वे सिद्धिं सम्यग्लभन्ति वै ॥ २९ ॥

29. Only the siddha knows the importance of these three and no one else; knowing these, the practitioner obtains all success.

गोपनीया प्रयत्नेन साधकैः सिद्धिमीप्सुभिः ।
अन्यथा च न सिद्धिः स्यान्मुद्राणामेष निश्चयः ॥ ३० ॥

30. This should be kept in great secrecy by the practitioner desirous of obtaining power; otherwise, it is certain that the coveted powers can never be obtained through the practice of Mudrâs.

(4.)—*Khechari.*

अथ खेचरीमुद्राकथनम् ।
भ्रुवोरन्तर्गतां दृष्टिं विधाय सुदृढां सुधीः ।
उपविश्यासने वज्रे नानोपद्रववर्जितः ॥
लम्बिकोर्ध्वं स्थिते गर्ते रसनां विपरीतगाम् ।
संयोजयेत्प्रयत्नेन सुधाकूपे विचक्षणः ।
मुद्रैषा खेचरी प्रोक्ता भक्तानामनुरोधतः ॥ ३१ ॥

31. The wise Yogi, sitting in *vajrâsana* posture, in a place free from all disturbance, should firmly fix his gaze on the spot in the middle of the two eyebrows,; and reversing the tongue backwards, fix it in the hollow under the epi-glottis, placing it with great care on the mouth of the well of nectar, (*i.e.* closing up the air passage). This mudrâ, described by me at the request of my devotees, is the Khechari-Mudrâ.

सिद्धीनां जननी ह्येषा मम प्राणाधिकप्रिया ।
निरन्तरकृताभ्यासात्पीयूषं प्रत्यहं पिबेत् ॥
तेन विग्रहसिद्धिः स्यान्मृत्युमातङ्गकेसरी ॥ ३२ ॥

32. O, my beloved! know this to be the source of all success, always practising it let him drink the ambrosia daily. By this he obtains *vigraha-siddhi* (power over the microcosm), even as a lion over the elephant of death.

अपवित्रः पवित्रो वा सर्वावस्थां गतोऽपिवा ।
खेचरी यस्य शुद्धा तु स शुद्धो नात्र संशयः ॥ ३३ ॥

33. Whether pure or impure, in whatever condition one may be, if success be obtained in Khechari, he becomes pure. There is no doubt of it.

क्षणार्धं कुरुते यस्तु तीर्त्वा पापमहार्णवम् ।
दिव्यभोगान्प्रभुक्त्वा च सत्कुले स प्रजायते ॥ ३४ ॥

34. He who practises it even for a moment crosses the great ocean of sins, and having enjoyed the pleasures of Deva-world is born into a noble family.

मुद्रैषा खेचरी यस्तु स्वस्थचित्तो ह्यतन्द्रितः ।
शतब्रह्मगतेनापि क्षणार्धं मन्यते हि सः ॥ ३५ ॥

35. He who practises this Khechari-Mudrâ calmly and without laziness counts as seconds the period of hundred Brahmâs.

गुरूपदेशतो मुद्रां यो वेत्ति खेचरीमिमाम् ।
नानापापरतो धीमान् स याति परमां गतिम् ॥ ३६ ॥

36. He knows this Khechari-Mudrâ according to the instructions of his Guru, obtains the highest end, though immersed in great sins.

सा प्राणसदृशी मुद्रा यस्मिन्कस्मिन्न दीयते ।
प्रच्छाद्यते प्रयत्नेन मुद्रेयं सुरपूजिते ॥ ३७ ॥

37. O, ye adored of gods! this Mudrâ, dear as life, should not be given to everybody; it should be kept concealed with great care.

(5.)—*Jâlandhara.*

अथ जालन्धरबन्ध ।
बद्ध्वागलशिराजालं हृदये चिबुकं न्यसेत् ।
बन्धोजालन्धरः प्रोक्तो देवानामपि दुर्लभः ॥
नाभिस्थवह्निर्जन्तूनां सहस्रकमलच्युतम् ।
पिबेत्पीयूषविस्तारं तदर्थं बन्धयेदिमम् ॥ ३८ ॥

38. Having contracted the muscles of the throat press the chin on the breast. This is said to be the Jâlandhara-Mudrâ. Even gods reckon it as inestimable. The fire in the region of the navel (*i.e.*, the gastric juice) drinks the nectar which exudes out of the thousand-petalled lotus. [In order to prevent the nectar to be thus consumed], he should practise this Bandha.

बन्धेनानेन पीयूषं स्वयं पिबति बुद्धिमान् ।
अमरत्वञ्च सम्प्राप्य मोदते भुवनत्रये ॥ ३९ ॥

39. Through this Bandha, the wise Yogi himself drinks the nectar, and, obtaining immortality, enjoys the three-worlds.

जालन्धरो बन्ध एष सिद्धानां सिद्धिदायकः ।
अभ्यासः क्रियते नित्यं योगिना सिद्धिमिच्छता ॥ ४० ॥

40. This Jâlandhara-Bandha is the giver of success to the practitioner; the Yogi desirous of success should practise it daily.

(6.)—*Mula-Bandha.*

अथ मूलबन्धः ।
पादमूलेन संपीड्य गुदमार्गं सुयन्त्रितम् ।
बलादपानमाकृष्य क्रमादूर्ध्वं सुचारयेत् ।
कल्पितोऽयं मूलबन्धो जरामरणनाशनः ॥ ४१ ॥

41. Pressing well the anus with the heel, forcibly draw upwards the *apâna vâyu* slowly by practice. This is described as the Mula-Bandha—the destroyer of decay and death.

अपानप्राणयोरैक्यं प्रकरोत्यधिकल्पितम् ।
बन्धेनानेन सुतरां योनिमुद्रा प्रसिद्ध्यति ॥ ४२ ॥

42. If, in the course of the practice of this Mudrâ, the Yogi can unite the *apâna* with the *prâṇa vâyu*, then it becomes of course the Yoni-Mudrâ.

सिद्धायां योनिमुद्रायां किं न सिध्यति भूतले ।
बन्धस्यास्य प्रसादेन गगने विजितालसः ॥
पद्मासने स्थितो योगी भुवमुत्सृज्य वर्तते ॥ ४३ ॥

43. He who has accomplished Yoni-Mudrâ, what can he not accomplish in this world. Sitting in the *padmâsana* posture, free from idleness, the Yogi, leaving the ground, moves through the air, by virtue of this Mudrâ.

सुगुप्ते निर्जने देशे बन्धमेनं समभ्यसेत् ।
संसारसागरं तर्तुं यदीच्छेद्योगि पुंगवः ॥ ४४ ॥

44. If the wise Yogi is desirous of crossing the ocean of the world, let him practise this Bandha in secret, in a retired place.

(7.) *Viparit-karaṇa.*

अथ विपरीतकरणी मुद्रा ।
भूतले स्वशिरोदत्त्वा खे नयेच्चरणद्वयम् ।
विपरीतकृतिश्चैषा सर्वतन्त्रेषु गोपिता ॥ ४५ ॥

45. Putting the head on the ground, let him stretch out his legs upwards, moving them round and round. This is *Viparit-karaṇa*, kept secret in all the Tantras.

एतद्यः कुरुते नित्यमभ्यासं याममात्रतः ।
मृत्युं जयति स योगी प्रलये नापि सीदति ॥ ४६ ॥

46. The Yogi who practises it daily for three hours, conquers death, and is not destroyed even in the Pralaya.

कुरुतेऽमृतपानं यः सिद्धानां समतामियात् ।
स सेव्यः सर्वलोकानां बन्धमेनं करोति यः ॥ ४७ ॥

47. He who drinks nectar becomes equal to Siddhas; he who practises this Bandha becomes an adept among all creatures.

(8.)—*Uḍḍâna-bandha.*

नाभेरूर्ध्वमधश्चापि तानं पश्चिममाचरेत् ।
उड्डयानबंध एष स्यात्सर्वदुःखौघनाशनः ॥
उदरे पश्चिमं तानं नाभेरूर्ध्वं तु कारयेत् ।
उड्डानाख्योऽत्र बन्धोयं मृत्युमातङ्गकेसरी ॥ ४८ ॥

48. When the intestines above and below the navel are brought to the left side, it is called Uḍḍâna-Bandha—the destroyer of all sins and sorrows. The left side viscera of the abdominal cavity should be brought above the navel. This is Uḍḍana-Bandha, the lion of the elephant of death.

नित्यं यः कुरुते योगी चतुर्वारं दिने दिने ।
तस्य नाभेस्तु शुद्धिः स्याद्येन सिद्धो भवेन्मरुत् ॥ ४९ ॥

49. The Yogi, who always practises it four times a day, purifies thereby his navel, through which the winds are purified.

षण्मासमभ्यसन्योगी मृत्युं जयति निश्चितम् ।
तस्योदराग्निर्ज्वलति रसवृद्धिः प्रजायते ॥ ५० ॥

50. By practising it for six months, the Yogi certainly conquers death; the gastric fire is kindled, and there takes place an increase of the fluids of the body.

अनेन सुतरां सिद्धिर्विग्रहस्य प्रजायते ।
रोगाणां संक्षयश्चापि योगिनो भवति ध्रुवम् ॥ ५१ ॥

51. Through this, consequently, the *vigrahasiddhi* is also obtained. All the diseases of the Yogi are certainly destroyed by it.

गुरोर्लब्ध्वा प्रयत्नेन साधयेत्तु विचक्षणः ।
निर्जने सुस्थिते देशे बन्धं परम दुर्लभम् ॥ ५२ ॥

52. Having learnt the method from the Guru, the wise Yogi should practise it with great care. This most inacessible Mudrâ should be practised in a retired and undisturbed place.

(10.)—*Shakti-châlan.*

अथ शक्तिचालनमुद्रा ।
आधारकमले सुप्तां चालयेत्कुण्डलीं दृढाम् ।
अपानवायुमारुह्य बलादाकृष्य बुद्धिमान् ।
शक्तिचालनमुद्रेयं सर्वशक्तिप्रदायिनी ॥ ५३ ॥

53. Let the wise Yogi forcibly and firmly draw up the goddess Kuṇḍali sleeping in the *âdhâr* lotus, by means of the *apâna vâyu.* This is Shakti-Châlan Mudrâ, the giver of all powers.

शक्तिचालनमेवं हि प्रत्यहं यः समाचरेत् ।
आयुर्वृद्धिर्भवेत्तस्य रोगाणां च विनाशनम् ॥ ५४ ॥

54. He who practises this Shakti-Châlan daily, gets increase of life and destruction of diseases.

विहाय निद्रां भुजगी स्वयमूर्ध्वं भवेत्खलु ।
तस्मादभ्यासनं कार्यं योगिना सिद्धमिच्छता ॥ ५५ ॥

55. Leaving sleep, the serpent (*i.e.* the Kuṇḍali) herself goes up; therefore let the Yogi desirous of power practise this.

यः करोति सदाभ्यासं शक्तिचालनमुत्तमम् ।
येन विग्रहसिद्धिः स्यादणिमादिगुणप्रदा ।
गुरूपदेशविधिना तस्य मृत्युभयं कुतः ॥ ५६ ॥

56. He who practises always this best Shakti-Châlan according to the instructions of his guru, obtains the *vigraha-siddhi*, which gives the powers of *animâ*, etc., and has no fear of death.

मुहूर्तद्वयपर्यन्तं विधिना शक्तिचालनम् ।
यः करोति प्रयत्नेन तस्य सिद्धिरदूरतः ।
युक्तासनेन कर्तव्यं योगिभिः शक्तिचालनम् ॥ ५७ ॥

57. He who practises the Shakti-Châlan properly for two seconds, and with care, is very near to success. This Mudrâ should be practised by the Yogi in the proper posture.

एतत्तु मुद्रादशकं न भूतं न भविष्यति ।
एकैकाभ्यासने सिद्धिः सिद्धो भवति नान्यथा ॥ ५८ ॥

58. These are the ten Mudrâs whose equal there never was nor ever shall be: through the practice of any one of them, a person becomes a siddha and obtains success.

इति श्रीशिवसंहितायां हरगौरीसंवादे मुद्राकथनं नाम चतुर्थपटलः समाप्तः ॥ ४ ॥

[Vajroṇḍi Mudrâ described in this chapter in the original is omitted here, as it is an obscene practice indulged in by low class Tantrists. Translator.]

CHAPTER V.

अथ पञ्चमः पटलः ॥

श्री देव्युवाच ॥ ब्रूहि मे वाक्यमीशान परमार्थधियं प्रति ।
ये विघ्नाः सन्ति लोकानां वद मे प्रिय शङ्कर ॥ १ ॥

Pârvati.—O Lord, O beloved Shankar! tell me, for the sake of those whose minds search after the supreme end, *the obstacles and the hindances to Yoga.*

ईश्वर उवाच ॥ शृणु देवि प्रवक्ष्यामि यथा विघ्नाः स्थिताः सदा ।
मुक्तिं प्रति नराणाञ्च भोगः परमबन्धनः ॥ २ ॥

2. *Śiva.*—Hear, O Goddess! I shall tell thee, all the obstacles that stand in the path of Yoga. For the attainment of emancipation, enjoyments (*bhoga*) are the greatest of all impediments.

Bhoga (enjoyment).

अथ भोगरूपयोगविघ्नकथनम् ।
नारी शय्यासनं वस्त्रं धनमस्य विडम्बनम् ।
ताम्बूलंभक्ष्ययानानि राज्यैश्वर्यविभूतयः ।
हैमं रौप्यं तथा ताम्रं रत्नञ्चागुरुधेनवः ।
पाण्डित्यं वेदशास्त्राणि नृत्यं गीतं विभूषणम् ।
वंशी वीणा मृदङ्गाश्च गजेन्द्रश्चाश्ववाहनम् ।
दारापत्यानि विषया विघ्ना एते प्रकीर्त्तिताः ।
भोगरूपा इमे विघ्ना धर्मरूपानिमाञ्छृणु ॥ ३ ॥

3. Women, beds, seats, dresses, and riches are obstacles to Yoga. Betels, dainty dishes, carriages, kingdoms, lordliness and powers; gold, silver, as well as copper, gems, aloe wood, and kine; *learning* the Vedas and the Sâstras; dancing, singing and ornaments; harp, flute and drum; riding on elephants and horses; wives and children, worldly enjoyments; all these are so many impediments. These are the obstacles which arise from bhoga (enjoyment). Hear now the impediments which arise from ritualistic religion.

Dharma (ritualism of Religion.)

अथ धर्मरूपयोगविघ्नकथनम् ।
स्नानं पूजाविधिर्होमं तथा मोक्षमयी स्थितिः ।
व्रतोपवासनियममौनमिन्द्रियनिग्रहः ।
ध्येयो ध्यानं तथा मन्त्रो दानं ख्यातिर्दिशासु च ।

वापीकूपतडागादिप्रासादारामकल्पना ।
यज्ञं चान्द्रायणं कृच्छ्रं तीर्थानि विविधानि च ।
दृश्यन्ते च इमे विघ्ना धर्मरूपेण संस्थिताः ॥ ४ ॥

4. The following are the obstacles which dharma interposes :—ablutions, worship of dieties, observing the sacred days of the moon, fire sacrifice, hankering after *moksha*, vows and penances, fasts, religious observances, silence, the ascetic practices, contemplation and the object of contemplation, *mantras*, and alms-giving, world-wide fame, excavating and endowing of tanks, wells, ponds, convents and groves ; sacrifices, vows of starvation, Châṇdrâyaṇa, and pilgrimages.

Jñâna (Knowledge-obstacles).

अथ ज्ञानरूपविघ्नकथनम् ।
यत्तु विघ्नं भवेज्ज्ञानं कथयामि वरानने ।
गोमुखं स्वासनं कृत्वा धौतिप्रक्षालनं च तत् ।
नाडीसञ्चारविज्ञानं प्रत्याहारनिरोधनम् ।
कुक्षिसंचालनं क्षिप्रं प्रवेश इन्द्रियाध्वना ।
नाडीकर्माणि कल्याणि भोजनं श्रूयतां मम ॥ ५ ॥

5. Now I shall describe, O Pârvati, the obstacles which arise from knowledge. Sitting in the *Gomukh* posture and practising Dhauti (washing the intestines by Haṭha Yoga). Knowledge of the distribution of the nâḍis (the vessels of the human body), learning of pratyâhâra (subjugation of senses), trying to awaken the Kuṇḍalini force, by moving quickly the belly (a process of Haṭha Yoga), entering into the path of the *indriyas*, and knowledge of the action of the *nâḍis*; these are the obstacles. Now listen to the mistaken notions of diet, O Pârvati.

नवधातुरसं छिन्धि शुण्ठिकास्ताडयेत्पुनः ।
एककालं समाधिः स्याल्लिंगभूतमिदं शृणु ॥ ६ ॥

6. That *samâdhi* (trance) can be at once induced by drinking certain new chemical essences and by eating certain kinds of food, is a mistake. Now hear about the mistaken notion of the influence of company.

सङ्गमं गच्छ साधूनां संकोचं भज दुर्जनात् ।
प्रवेशनिर्गमे वायोर्गुरुलघुं विलोकयेत् ॥ ७ ॥

7. "Keep the company of the virtuous, and avoid that of the vicious" (is a mistaken notion). Measuring of the heaviness and lightness of the inspired and expired air (is an erroneous idea).

पिण्डस्थं रूपसंस्थञ्च रूपस्थं रूपवर्जितम् ।
ब्रह्मैतस्मिन्मतावस्था हृदयञ्च प्रशाम्यति ।
इत्येते कथिता विघ्ना ज्ञानरूपे व्यवस्थिताः ॥ ८ ॥

8. Brahman is in the body or He is the maker of form, or He has a form, or He has no form, or He is everything—all these consoling doctrines are obstacles. Such notions are impediments in the shape of Jnaña (knowledge).

Four Kinds of Yoga.

अथ चतुर्विधयोगकथनम् ।
मन्त्रयोगो हठश्चैव लययोगस्तृतीयकः ।
चतुर्थो राजयोगः स्यात्स द्विधाभाववर्जितः ॥ ९ ॥

9. The Yoga is of four kinds:—First Mantra-Yoga, second Haṭha-Yoga, third Laya-Yoga, fourth Raj-Yoga, which discards duality.

Sâdhaks (Aspirants).

चतुर्धा साधको ज्ञेयो मृदुमध्याधिमात्रकाः ।
अधिमात्रतमः श्रेष्ठो भवाब्धौ लंघनक्षमः ॥ १० ॥

10. Know that aspirants are of four orders:—mild, moderate, ardent and the most ardent—the best who can cross the ocean of the world.

(Mild) entitled to Mantra-Yoga.

अथ मृदुसाधकलक्षणम् ।
मन्दोत्साही सुसंमूढो व्याधिस्थो गुरुदूषकः ।
लोभी पापमतिश्चैव बह्वाशी वनिताश्रयः ॥
चपलः कातरो रोगी पराधीनोऽतिनिष्ठुरः ।
मन्दाचारो मन्दवीर्यो ज्ञातव्यो मृदुमानवः ॥
द्वादशाब्दे भवेत्सिद्धिरेतस्य यत्नतः परम् ।
मन्त्रयोगाधिकारी स ज्ञातव्यो गुरुणा ध्रुवम् ॥ ११ ॥

11. Men of small enterprise, oblivious, sickly and finding faults with their teachers; avaricious, sinful gourmands, and attached helplessly to their wives; fickle, timid, diseased, not independent, and cruel; those whose characters are bad and who are weak—know all the above to be mild sâdhaks. With great efforts such men succeed in twelve years; them the teacher should know fit for the Mantra-Yoga.

(Moderate) entitled to Laya-Yoga.

समबुद्धिः क्षमायुक्तः पुण्याकांक्षी प्रियंवदः ।
मध्यस्थः सर्वकार्येषु सामान्यः स्यान्न संशयः ॥
एतज्ज्ञात्वैव गुरुभिर्दीयते मुक्तितो लयः ॥ १२ ॥

12. Liberal-minded, merciful, desirous of virtue, sweet in their speech; who never go to extremes in any undertaking—these are the middling. These are to be initiated by the teacher in Laya-Yoga.

(Ardent) entitled to Haṭha Yoga

अथ अधिमात्रसाधकलक्षणम्
स्थिरबुद्धिर्लये युक्तः स्वाधीनो वीर्यवानपि ।
महाशयो दयायुक्तः क्षमावान् सत्यवानपि ॥
शूरो वयःस्थः श्रद्धावान् गुरुपादाब्जपूजकः ।
योगाभ्यासरतश्चैव ज्ञातव्यश्चाधिमात्रकः ॥
एतस्य सिद्धिः षड्वर्षे भवेदभ्यासयोगतः ।
एतस्मै दीयते धीरो हठयोगश्च साङ्गतः ॥ १३ ॥

13. Steady-minded, knowing the Laya-Yoga, independent, full of energy, magnanimous, full of sympathy, forgiving, truthful, courageous, full of faith, worshippers of the lotus-feet of their Gurus, engaged always in the practice of Yoga,—know such men to be adhimâtra. They obtain success in the practice of Yoga within six years, and ought to be initiated in Haṭha-Yoga and its branches.

(The most ardent) entitled to all Yogas

अथ अधिमात्रतमसाधकलक्षणम् ।
महावीर्यान्वितोत्साही मनोज्ञः शौर्यवानपि ।
शास्त्रज्ञोऽभ्यासशीलश्च निर्मोहश्च निराकुलः ॥
नवयौवनसम्पन्नो मिताहारी जितेंद्रियः ।
निर्भयश्च शुचिर्दक्षो दाता सर्वजनाश्रयः ॥
अधिकारी स्थिरो धीमान् यथेच्छावस्थितः क्षमी ।
सुशीलो धर्मचारी च गुप्तचेष्टः प्रियंवदः ॥
शास्त्रविश्वाससम्पन्नो देवता गुरुपूजकः ।
जनसंगविरक्तश्च महाव्याधि विवर्जितः ॥
अधिमात्रव्रतज्ञश्च सर्वयोगस्य साधकः ।
त्रिभिः संवत्सरैः सिद्धिरेतस्य नात्र संशयः ॥
सर्वयोगाधिकारी स नात्र कार्या विचारणा ॥ १४ ॥

14. Those who have the largest amount of energy, are enterprising, engaging, heroic, who know the śastras, and are persevering, *free from the effects of blind emotions*, and, not easily confused, who are in the prime of their youth, moderate in their diet, rulers of their senses, fearless, clean, skilful, charitable, a help to all; competent, firm, talented, contented, forgiving, good-natured, religious, *who keep their endeavours secret*, of sweet speech, peaceful, who have faith in scriptures and are worshippers

of God and Guru, who are averse to fritter away their time in society, and are free from any grievous malady, who are acquainted with the duties of the *adhimâtra*, and are the practitioners of every kind of Yoga— undoubtedly, they obtain success in three years; they are entitled to be initiated in all kinds of Yoga, without any hesitation.

Invocation of the shadow (pratikopâsana).

अथ प्रतीकोपासनम् ।
प्रतीकोपासना कार्या दृष्टादृष्टफलप्रदा ।
पुनाती दर्शनादत्र नात्र कार्या विचारणा ॥ १५ ॥

15. The invocation of Pratika (shadow) gives to the devotee the objects seen as well as unseen; undoubtedly, by its very sight, a man becomes pure.

गाढातपे स्वप्रतिबिम्बितेश्वरं निरीक्ष्य विस्फारितलोचनद्वयम् ।
यदा नभः पश्यति स्वप्रतीकं नभोङ्गणे तत्क्षणमेव पश्यति ॥ १६ ॥

16. In a clear sun-lit sky, behold with a steady gaze your own divine reflection; whenever this is seen even for a single second in the sky, you behold God at once in the sky.

प्रत्यहं पश्यते यो वै स्वप्रतीकं नभोङ्गणे ।
आयुर्वृद्धिर्भवेत्तस्य न मृत्युः स्यात्कदाचन ॥ १७ ॥

17. He who daily sees his shadow in the sky, will get his years increased and will never die an accidental death.

यदा पश्यति सम्पूर्णं स्वप्रतीकं नभोङ्गणे ।
तदा जयमवाप्नोति वायुं निर्जित्य सञ्चरेत् ॥ १८ ॥

18. When the shadow is seen fully reflected in the field of the sky, then he obtains victory; and conquering the vâyu, he goes everywhere.

How to invoke.

At the time of the rising sun, or by moon, let him steadily fix his gaze on the neck of the shadow he throws; then, after sometime, let him look into the sky; if he sees a full grey shadow in the sky, it is auspicious.

यः करोति सदाभ्यासं चात्मानं वन्दते परम् ।
पूर्णानन्दैकपुरुषं स्वप्रतीकप्रसादतः ॥ १९ ॥

19. He who always practises this and knows the Paramâtmâ, becomes fully happy, through the grace of his shadow.

यात्राकाले विवाहे च शुभे कर्मणि सङ्कटे।
पापक्षये पुण्यवृद्धौ प्रतीकोपासनञ्चरेत् ॥ २० ॥

20. At the time of commencing travel, marriage, or auspicious work, or when in trouble, it is of great use. This invocation of the shadow destroys sins and increases virtue.

निरन्तरकृताभ्यासादन्तरे पश्यति ध्रुवम्।
तदा मुक्तिमवाप्नोति योगी नियतमानसः ॥ २१ ॥

21. By practising it always, he begins at last to see it in his heart, and the persevering Yogi gets liberation.

Râj Yoga.

अंगुष्ठाभ्यामुभे श्रोत्रे तर्जनीभ्यां द्विलोचने।
नासारन्ध्रे च मध्याभ्यामनामाभ्यां मुखं दृढम् ॥
निरुध्य मारुतं योगी यदैव कुरुते भृशम्।
तदा लक्षणमात्मानं ज्योतीरूपं स पश्यति ॥ २२ ॥

22. Let him close the ears with his thumbs, the eyes with index fingers, the nostril with the middle fingers, and with the remaining four fingers let him press together the upper and lower lips. The Yogi, by having thus firmly confined the air, sees his soul in the shape of light.

तत्तेजो दृश्यते येन क्षणमात्रं निराकुलम्।
सर्वपापविनिर्मुक्तः स याति परमां गतिम् ॥ २३ ॥

23. When one sees, without obstruction, this light for even a moment, becoming free from sin, he reaches the highest end.

निरन्तरकृताभ्यासाद्योगी विगतकल्मषः।
सर्वदेहादि विस्मृत्य तदभिन्नः स्वयं गतः ॥ २४ ॥

24. The Yogi, free from sin, and practising this continually, forgets his physical, subtle and causal bodies, and becomes one with that soul.

यः करोति सदाभ्यासं गुप्ताचारेण मानवः।
स वै ब्रह्मविलीनः स्यात्पापकर्मरतो यदि ॥ २५ ॥

25. He who practises this in secrecy, is absorbed in the Brahman, though he had been engaged in sinful works.

गोपनीयः प्रयत्नेन सद्यः प्रत्ययकारकः।
निर्वाणदायको लोके योगोऽयं मम वल्लभः ॥
नादः संजायते तस्य क्रमेणाभ्यासतश्च वै ॥ २६ ॥

26. This should be kept secret; it at once produces conviction; it gives *nirvâna* to mankind. This is my most beloved Yoga. From practising this gradually, the Yogi begins to hear the mystic sounds (nâdas).

Anâhad Sounds.

मत्तभृङ्गवेणुवीणासदृशः प्रथमो ध्वनिः ।
एवमभ्यासतः पश्चात् संसारध्वान्तनाशनम् ॥
घण्टानादसमः पश्चात् ध्वनिर्मेघरवोपमः ।
ध्वनौ तस्मिन्मनो दत्त्वा यदा तिष्ठति निर्भयः ॥
तदा संजायते तस्य लयस्य मम वल्लभे ॥ २७ ॥

27. The first sound is like the hum of the honey-intoxicated bee, next that of a flute, then of a harp; after this, by the gradual practice of Yoga, the destroyer of the darkness of the world, he hears the sounds of ringing bells; then sounds like roar of thunder. When one fixes his full attention on this sound, being free from fear, he gets absorption, O my beloved!

तत्र नादे यदा चित्तं रमते योगिनो भृशम् ।
विस्मृत्य सकलं बाह्यं नादेन सह शाम्यति ॥ २८ ॥

28. When the mind of the Yogi is exceedingly engaged in this sound, he forgets all external things, and is absorbed in this sound.

एतदभ्यासयोगेन जित्वा सम्यग्गुणान्बहून् ।
सर्वारम्भपरित्यागी चिदाकाशे विलीयते ॥ २९ ॥

29. By this practice of Yoga he conquers all the three qualities (*i.e.*, good, bad and indifferent); and being free from all states, he is absorbed in *chidâkâs* (the ether of intelligence).

A Secret.

नासनं सिद्धसदृशं न कुम्भसदृशं बलम् ।
न खेचरीसमा मुद्रा न नादसदृशो लयः ॥ ३० ॥

30 There is no posture like that of *Siddhâsana*, no power like that of *Kumbha*, no *Mudrâ* like the *Khechari*, and no absorption like that of *nâda* (the mystic sound).

इदानीं कथयिष्यामि मुक्तस्यानुभवं प्रिये ।
यज्ज्ञात्वा लभते मुक्तिं पापयुक्तोपि साधकः ॥ ३१ ॥

31. Now I shall describe to thee, O dear, the foretaste of salvation, knowing which even the sinful aspirant may obtain salvation.

समभ्यर्च्येश्वरं सम्यक्कृत्वा च योगमुत्तमम् ।
गृह्णीयात्सुस्थितो भूत्वा गुरुं सन्तोष्य बुद्धिमान् ॥ ३२ ॥

32. Having adored the Lord God properly, and having completely performed the best of the Yogas, and being in a calm and steady state and posture, let the wise Yogi initiate himself into this Yoga by pleasing his Guru.

जीवादि सकलं वस्तु दत्त्वा योगविदं गुरुम्।
सन्तोष्यातिप्रयत्नेन योगोयं गृह्यते बुधैः ॥ ३३ ॥

33. Having given all his cattle and property to the Guru who knows Yoga, and having satisfied him with great care, let the wise man receive this initiation.

विप्रान्संतोष्य मेधावी नानामंगलसंयुतः।
ममालये शुचिर्भूत्वा प्रगृह्णीयाच्छुभात्मकम् ॥ ३४ ॥

34. Having pleased the Brâhmans (and priest), by giving them all kinds of good things, let the wise man receive this auspicious Yoga in my house (*i.e.*, the temple of Shiva) with purity of heart.

संन्यस्यानेन विधिना प्राक्तनं विग्रहादिकम्।
भूत्वा दिव्यवपुर्योगी गृह्णीयाद्वक्ष्यमाणकम् ॥ ३५ ॥

35. Having renounced by the above methods all his previous bodies (the results of his past karma), and being in his spiritual (or luminous) body, let the Yogi receive this highest Yoga.

पद्मासनस्थितो योगी जनसंगविवर्जितः।
विज्ञाननाडीद्वितयमङ्गुलीभ्यां निरोधयेत् ॥ ३६ ॥

36. Sitting in the padmâsana posture, renouncing the society of men, let the Yogi press the two *vijñâna nâdis* (the vessels of consciousness, perhaps coronal arteries) with his two fingers.

सिद्धेस्तदाविर्भवति सुखरूपी निरञ्जनः।
तस्मिन्परिश्रमः कार्यो येन सिद्धो भवेत्खलु ॥ ३७ ॥

37. By obtaining success in this, he becomes all happiness and unstained; therefore, let him endeavour with all his might, in order to ensure success.

यः करोति सदाभ्यासं तस्य सिद्धिर्न दूरतः।
वायुसिद्धिर्भवेत्तस्य क्रमादेव न संशयः ॥ ३८ ॥

38. He who practises this always, obtains success within a short time; he gets also *vâyu-siddhi* in course of time.

सकृद्यः कुरुते योगी पापौघं नाशयेद्ध्रुवम्।
तस्य स्यान्मध्यमे वायोः प्रवेशो नात्र संशयः ॥ ३९ ॥

39. The Yogi, who does it even once, verily destroys all sins; and undoubtedly in him the *vâyus* enter the middle channel.

एतदभ्यासशीलो यः स योगी देवपूजितः।
अणिमादिगुणाँल्लब्ध्वा विचरेद्भुवनत्रये ॥ ४० ॥

40. The Yogi who practises this with perseverance is worshipped even by gods; he receives the psychic powers of *animâ*, *laghimâ* etc., and can go everywhere, throughout the three worlds, at pleasure.

येा यथास्यानिलाभ्यासात्तद्भवेत्तस्य विग्रहः ।
तिष्ठेदात्मनि मेधावी संयुतः क्रीडते भृशम् ॥ ४१ ॥

41. According to the strength of one's practice in commanding the *vâyu*, he gets command over his body; the wise, remaining in the spirit, enjoys the world in the present body.

एतद्योगं परं गोप्यं न देयं यस्य कस्यचित् ।
यः प्रमाणैः समायुक्तस्तमेव कथ्यते ध्रुवम् ॥ ४२ ॥

42. This Yoga is a great secret, and not to be given to every body; it might be revealed to him only, in whom all the qualifications of a Yogi are perceived.

Various kinds of Dhâranâ.

येागी पद्मासने तिष्ठेत्कण्ठकूपे यदा स्मरन् ।
जिह्वां कृत्वा तालुमूले क्षुत्पिपासा निवर्तते ॥४३॥

43. Let the Yogi seat himself in the Padmâsana, and fix his attention on the cavity of the throat, let him place his tongue at the base of the palate; by this he will extinguish hunger and thirst.

कण्ठकूपादधः स्थाने कूर्मनाड्यस्ति शोभना ।
तस्मिन् येागी मने दत्त्वा चित्तस्थैर्यं लभेद्भृशम् ॥ ४४ ॥

44. Below the cavity of the throat, there is a beautiful *nâḍi* (vessel) called *kurma*; when the Yogi fixes his attention on it, he acquires great concentration of the thinking principle (chitta).

शिरः कपाले रुद्राक्षं विवरं चिन्तयेद्यदा ।
तदा ज्योतिः प्रकाशः स्याद्विद्युत्पुञ्जसमप्रभः ।
एतच्चिन्तनमात्रेण पापानां संक्षयेा भवेत् ।
दुराचारेाऽपि पुरुषेा लभते परमं पदम् ॥ ४५ ॥

45. When the Yogi constantly thinks that he has got a third ye—the eye of Shiva—in the middle of his forehead, he then perceives a fire brilliant like lightning. By contemplating on this light, all sins are destroyed, and even the most wicked person obtains the highest end.

अहर्निशं यदा चिन्तां तत्करोति विचक्षणः ।
सिद्धानां दर्शनं तस्य भाषणञ्च भवेद्ध्रुवम् ॥ ४६ ॥

46. If the experienced Yogi thinks of this light day and night, he sees the Siddhas (adepts), and can certainly converse with them.

तिष्ठन् गच्छन् स्वपन् भुञ्जन् ध्यायेच्छून्यमहर्निशम् ।
तदाकाशमयो योगी चिदाकाशे विलीयते ॥ ४७ ॥

47. He who contemplates on *śunya* (void or vacuum or space), while walking or standing, dreaming or waking, becomes altogether etherial, and is absorbed in the *chid* âkâśa.

एतज्ज्ञानं सदा कार्यं योगिना सिद्धिमिच्छता ।
निरन्तरकृताभ्यासान्मम तुल्यो भवेद्ध्रुवम् ॥
एतज्ज्ञानबलाद्योगी सर्वेषां वल्लभो भवेत् ॥ ४८ ॥

48. The Yogi, desirous of success, should always obtain this knowledge; by habitual exercise he becomes equal to me; through the force of this knowledge, he becomes the beloved of all.

सर्वान् भूतान् जयं कृत्वा निराशीरपरिग्रहः ।
नासाग्रे दृश्यते येन पद्मासनगतेन वै ॥
मनसो मरणं तस्य खेचरत्वं प्रसिद्ध्यति ॥ ४९ ॥

49. Having conquered all the elements, and being void of all hopes and worldly connections, when the Yogi sitting in the Padmâsana, fixes his gaze on the tip of the nose, his mind becomes dead and he obtains the spiritual power called *Khechari*.

ज्योतिः पश्यति योगीन्द्रः शुद्धं शुद्धाचलोपमम् ।
तत्राभ्यासबलेनैव स्वयं तद्रक्षको भवेत् ॥ ५० ॥

50. The great Yogi beholds light, pure as holy mountain (Kailâs), and through the force of his exercise in it, he becomes the lord and guardian of the light.

उत्तानशयने भूमौ सुप्त्वा ध्यायन्निरन्तरम् ।
सद्यः श्रमविनाशाय स्वयं योगी विचक्षणः ।
शिरः पश्चात्तु भागस्य ध्याने मृत्युञ्जयो भवेत् ॥
भ्रू मध्ये दृष्टिमात्रेण ह्यपरः परिकीर्तितः ॥ ५१ ॥

51. Stretching himself on the ground, let him contemplate on this light; by so doing all his weariness and fatigue are destroyed. By contemplating on the back part of his head, he becomes the conqueror of death. (We have described before the effect of fixing one's attention on the space between the two eyebrows, so it need not be enumerated here).

चतुर्विधस्य चान्नस्य रसस्त्रेधा विभज्यते ।
तत्र सारतमो लिंगदेहस्य परिपोषकः ॥
सप्तधातुमयं पिण्डमेती पुष्णाति मध्यगः ॥५२॥

52. Of the four kinds of food (*i.e.*, that which is chewed, that which is sucked, that which is licked and that which is drunk), which a man takes, the chyle fluid is converted into three parts. The best part (or the finest extract of food) goes to nourish the *linga sharira* or subtle body (the seat of force). The second or the middle part goes to nourish this gross body composed of seven *dhâtus* (humours)

याति विण्मूत्ररूपेण तृतीयः सप्ततो बहिः ॥
आद्यभागद्वयं नाड्यः प्रोक्तास्ताः सकला अपि ।
पोषयन्ति वपुर्वायुमापादतलमस्तकम् ॥ ५३ ॥

53. The third or the most inferior part goes out of the body in the shape of excrement and urine. The first two essences of food are found in the *nâḍis*, and being carried by them, they nourish the body from head to foot.

नाडीभिराभिः सर्वाभिर्वायुः सञ्चरते यदा ।
तदैवायरसो देहे साम्येनेह प्रवर्तते ॥ ५४ ॥

54. When the *vâyu* moves through all the *nâḍis*, then, owing to this *vâyu* (oxygen?), the fluids of the body get extraordinary force and energy.

चतुर्दशानां तत्रेह व्यापारे मुख्यभागतः ।
ता अनुग्रत्वहीनाश्च प्राणसञ्चारनाडिकाः ॥ ५५ ॥

55. The most important of these *nâḍis* are fourteen, distributed in different parts of the body and performing various functions. They are either weak or strong, and the *prâṇa* (vitality) flows through them.

The six Chakras.

Mulâdhâr Chakra.

गुदाद्व्यंगुलतश्चोर्ध्वं मेढ्रैकांगुलतस्त्वधः ।
एवञ्चास्ति समं कन्दं समताश्चतुरंगुलम् ॥ ५६ ॥

56. Two fingers above the rectum and two fingers below the *linga*, four fingers in width, is a space like a bulbous root.

पश्चिमाभिमुखी योनिर्गुदमेढ्रान्तरालगा ।
तत्र कन्दं समाख्यातं तत्रास्ति कुण्डली सदा ॥
संवेष्ट्य सकला नाडीः सार्द्धत्रिकुटिलाकृतिः ।
मुखे निवेश्य सा पुच्छं सुषुम्णाविवरे स्थिता ॥ ५७ ।

57. Between this space is the *yoni* having its face towards the back; that space is called the root; there dwells the goddess *Kuṇḍalini*. It surrounds all the *nâḍis*, and has three coils and a half; and catching its tail in its own mouth, it rests in the hole of the *Sushumnâ*.

सुप्ता नागोपमा ह्येषा स्फुरन्ती प्रभया स्वया।
अहिवत्सन्धिसंस्थाना वाग्देवी बीजसंज्ञिका॥ ५८॥

58. It sleeps there like a serpent, and is luminous by its own light. Like a serpent it lives between the joints; it is the goddess of speech, and is called the seed (*vija*).

ज्ञेया शक्तिरियं विष्णोर्निर्भरा स्वर्णभास्वरा।
सत्त्वं रजस्तमश्चेति गुणत्रयप्रसूतिका॥ ५९॥

59. Full of energy, and like burning gold, know this Kuṇḍalini to be the power (*shakti*) of *Vishnu*; it is the mother of the three qualities—sattwa (rhythm), rajas (energy) and tamas (inertia).

तत्र बन्धूकपुष्पाभं कामबीजं प्रकीर्तितम्।
कलहेमसमं योगे प्रयुक्ताक्षररूपिणम्॥ ६०॥

60. There, beautiful like the *Bandhuk* flower, is placed the seed of love (क्लीँ); it is brilliant like burnished gold, and is described in Yoga as eternal.

सुषुम्णापि च संश्लिष्टा बीजं तत्र वरं स्थितम्।
शरच्चंद्रनिभं तेजस्स्वयमेतत्स्फुरत्स्थितम्॥
सूर्यकोटिप्रतीकाशं चन्द्रकोटिसुशीतलम्।
एतत्त्रयं मिलित्वैव देवी त्रिपुरभैरवी॥
बीजसंज्ञं परंतेजस्तदेव परिकीर्तितम्॥ ६१॥

61. The *Sushumnâ* also embraces it, and the beautiful seed is there; there it rests shining brilliantly like the autumnal moon, with the luminosity of millions of suns, and the coolness of millions of moons. The goddess Tripûra Bhairavî has these three (fire, sun, and moon) taken together, and collectively she is called the *vija*. It is also called the great energy.

क्रियाविज्ञानशक्तिभ्यां युतं यत्परितो भ्रमत्।
उत्तिष्ठद्विशतस्त्वम्भः सूक्ष्मं शोणशिखायुतम्॥
योनिस्थं तत्परं तेजः स्वयंभूलिंगसंस्थितम्॥ ६२॥

62. It (*vija*) is endowed with the powers of action (motion) and sensation, and circulates throughout the body. It is subtle, and has a flame of fire; sometimes it rises up, and at other times it falls down into the water. This is the great energy which rests in the perinaeum, and is called the *swayambhu-linga* (the self-born).

आधारपद्ममेतद्धि योनिर्यस्यास्ति कन्दतः।
परिस्फुरद्वादिसान्तचतुर्वर्णं चतुर्दलम्॥ ६३॥

63. All this is called the *âdhâr-padma* (the support lotus), and the four petals of it are designated by the letters व (v) श (ś), ष (ṣ), स (s).

कुलाभिधं सुवर्णाभं स्वयम्भूलिङ्गसंगतम् ।
द्विरण्डो यत्र सिद्धोऽस्ति डाकिनी यत्र देवता ॥
तत्पद्ममध्यगा योनिस्तत्र कुण्डलिनी स्थिता ।
तस्या ऊर्ध्वे स्फुरत्तेजः कामबीजं भ्रमन्मतम् ॥
यः करोति सदा ध्यानं मूलाधारे विचक्षणः ।
तस्य स्याद्दार्दुरी सिद्धिर्भूमित्यागक्रमेण वै ॥ ६४ ॥

64. Near this *Swayambhu-linga* is a golden region called *Kula* (family); its presiding adept is called *Dviraṇda*, and its presiding goddess called *Dâkini*. In the centre of that lotus is the *Yoni* where resides the *Kuṇḍalini*; the circulating bright energy above that, is called *kâma-vija* (the seed of love). The wise man who always contemplates on this *Mulâdhâr* obtains *Dârduri-siddhi* (the frog-jump power); and by degrees he can altogether leave the ground (*i.e.*, rise in the air).

वपुषः कान्तिरुत्कृष्टा जठराग्निविवर्धनम् ।
आरोग्यञ्च पटुत्वञ्च सर्वज्ञत्वञ्च जायते ॥ ६५ ॥

65. The brilliancy of the body is increased, the gastric fire becomes powerful, and freedom from disease, cleverness, and omniscience ensue.

भूतं भव्यं भविष्यञ्च वेत्ति सर्वं सकारणम् ।
अश्रुतान्यपि शास्त्राणि सरहस्यं भवेद्ध्रुवम् ॥ ६६ ॥

66. He knows what has been, what is happening, and what is to be, together with their causes; he masters the unheard of sciences together with their mysteries.

वक्त्रे सरस्वती देवी सदा नृत्यति निर्भरम् ।
मन्त्रसिद्धिर्भवेत्तस्य जपादेव न संशयः ॥ ६७ ॥

67. On his tongue always dances the goddess of learning, he obtains *mantra-siddhi* (success in mantras), through constant repetition only.

जरामरणदुःखौघान्नाशयति गुरोर्वचः ।
इदं ध्यानं सदा कार्यं पवनाभ्यासिना परम् ।
ध्यानमात्रेण योगीन्द्रो मुच्यते सर्वकिल्बिषात् ॥ ६८ ॥

68. This is the dictum of the Guru:—"It destroys old age, death, and troubles innumerable." The practitioner of prâṇâyâma ought always to meditate upon it; by its very contemplation, the great Yogi is freed from all sins.

मूलपद्मं यदा ध्यायेद्योगी स्वयम्भुलिङ्गकम् ।
तदा तत्क्षणमात्रेण पापौघं नाशयेद्ध्रुवम् ॥ ६९ ॥

69. When the Yogi contemplates this *Mulâdhâr* lotus—the *Swayambhu-linga*—then, undoubtedly, at that very moment, all his sins are destroyed.

यं यं कामयते चित्ते तं तं फलमवाप्नुयात् ।
निरन्तरकृताभ्यासात्तं पश्यति विमुक्तिदम् ॥
बहिरभ्यन्तरे श्रेष्ठं पूजनीयं प्रयत्नतः ।
ततः श्रेष्ठतमं ह्येतन्नान्यदस्ति मतं मम ॥ ७० ॥

70. Whatever the mind desires, he gets; by habitual exercise he sees him, who gives salvation, who is the best both in and out, and who is to be worshipped with great care. Better than Him, I know none.

आत्मसंस्थं शिवं त्यक्त्वा बहिःस्थं यः समर्चयेत् ।
हस्तस्थं पिण्डमुत्सृज्य भ्रमते जीविताशया ॥ ७१ ॥

71. He who, leaving the Śiva (God) who is inside, worships that which is outside (*viz.*, worships external forms), is like one who throws away the sweetmeat in his hand, and wanders away in search of food.

आत्मलिंगार्चनं कुर्यादनालस्यं दिने दिने ।
तस्य स्यात्सकला सिद्धिर्नात्र कार्या विचारणा ॥ ७२ ॥

72. Let one thus meditate daily, without negligence, on his own *Swayambhu-linga*; and have no doubts that from this will come all powers.

निरन्तरकृताभ्यासात्षण्मासैः सिद्धिमाप्नुयात् ।
तस्य वायुप्रवेशोपि सुषुम्णायाम्भवेद्ध्रुवम् ॥ ७३ ॥

73. By habitual exercise, he gets success in six months; and undoubtedly his *vâyu* enters the middle channel (the *Sushumnâ*).

मनोजयञ्च लभते वायुबिन्दुविधारणात् ।
ऐहिकामुष्मिकीसिद्धिर्भवेन्नैवात्र संशयः ॥ ७४ ॥

74, He conquers the mind, and can restrain his breath and his semen; then he gets success in this as well as the other world, without doubt.

2. *Swâdhisthân Chakra. (Prostatic Plexus).*

अथ स्वाधिष्ठानचक्रविवरणम् ।
द्वितीयन्तु सरोजञ्च लिंगमूले व्यवस्थितम् ।
बादिलान्तं च षड्वर्णं परिभास्वरषड्दलम् ॥
स्वाधिष्ठानाभिधं तत्तु पंकजं शोणरूपकम् ।
बालाख्यो यत्र सिद्धोऽस्ति देवी यत्रास्ति राकिणी ॥ ७५ ॥

75. The second Chakra is situated at the base of the organ. It has six petals designated by the letters b, bh, m, y, r, l. Its stalk is

called Swâdhisthân, the colour of the lotus is blood-red, its presiding adept is called Bâlâ, and its goddess, Râkini.

यो ध्यायति सदा दिव्यं स्वाधिष्ठानारविन्दकम् ।
तस्य कामाङ्गनाः सर्वा भजन्ते काममोहिताः ॥ ७६ ॥

76. He who daily contemplates on this *Swâdhisthân lotus*, becomes an object of love and adoration to all beautiful goddesses.

विविधञ्चाश्रुतं शास्त्रं निःशङ्को वै भवेद्ध्रुवम् ।
सर्वरोगविनिर्मुक्तो लोके चरति निर्भयः ॥ ७७ ॥

77. He fearlessly recites the various Śâstras and sciences unknown to him before; becomes free from all diseases, and moves throughout the universe fearlessly.

मरणं खाद्यते तेन स केनापि न खाद्यते ।
तस्य स्यात्परमा सिद्धिरणिमादिगुणप्रदा ॥
वायुः सञ्चरते देहे रसवृद्धिर्भवेद्ध्रुवम् ।
आकाशपङ्कजगलत्पीयूषमपि वर्द्धते ॥ ७८ ॥

78. Death is eaten by him, he is eaten by none; he obtains the highest psychic powers like *animâ, laghimâ,* etc. The *vâyu* moves equably throughout his body; the humours of his body also are increased; the ambrosia exuding from the etherial lotus also increases in him.

3. *Maṇipur Chakra.*

अथ मणिपूरचक्रविवरणम् ।
तृतीयं पङ्कजं नाभौ मणिपूरकसंज्ञकम् ।
दशारंडादिफान्तार्णं शोभितं हेमवर्णकम् ॥ ७९ ॥

79. The third Chakra, called Maṇipur, is situated near the navel; it is of golden color, having ten petals designated by the letters d, ḍh, ṇ, t, th, d, dh, n, p, ph.

रुद्राख्यो यत्र सिद्धोऽस्ति सर्वमङ्गलदायकः ।
तत्रस्था लाकिनी नाम्नी देवी परमधार्मिका ॥ ८० ॥

80. Its presiding adept is called Rudra—the giver of all auspicious things, and the presiding goddess of this place is called the most sacred Lâkini.

तस्मिन् ध्यानं सदा योगी करोति मणिपूरके ।
तस्य पातालसिद्धिः स्यान्निरन्तरसुखावहा ॥
ईप्सितञ्च भवेल्लोके दुःखरोगविनाशनम् ।
कालस्य वञ्चनञ्चापि परदेहप्रवेशनम् ॥ ८१ ॥

81. When the Yogi contemplates on the Maṇipur lotus, he gets the power called the *pâtâl-siddhi*—the giver of constant happiness. He becomes lord of desires, destroys sorrows and diseases, cheats death, and can enter the body of another.

आम्बूनदादिकरणं सिद्धानां दर्शनं भवेत् ।
ओषधीदर्शनञ्चापि निधीनां दर्शनं भवेत् ॥ ८२ ॥

82. He can make gold, etc., see the adepts (clairvoyantly), discover medicines for diseases, and see hidden treasures.

4. *Anâhat Chakra.*

हृदयेऽनाहतं नाम चतुर्थं पङ्कजं भवेत् ।
कादिठान्तार्णसंस्थानं द्वादशारसमन्वितम् ॥
अतिशोणं वायुबीजं प्रसादस्थानमीरितम् ॥ ८३ ॥

83. In the heart, is the fourth Chakra, the Anâhat. It has twelve petals designated by the letters k, kh, g, gh, ṅ, ch, chh, j, jh, ñ, ṭ, ṭh. Its color is deep blood-red; it has the seed of *vâyu*, यँ, and is a very pleasant spot.

पद्मस्थं तत्परं तेजो बाणलिंगं प्रकीर्तितम् ।
यस्य स्मरणमात्रेण दृष्टादृष्टफलं लभेत् ॥ ८४ ॥

84. In this lotus is a flame called *vâṇlinga*; by contemplating on this, one gets objects of the seen and the unseen universe.

सिद्धः पिनाकी यत्रास्ते काकिनी यत्र देवता ।
एतस्मिन्सततं ध्यानं हृत्पाथोजे करोति यः ॥
क्षुभ्यन्ते तस्य कान्ता वै कामार्ता दिव्ययोषितः ॥ ८५ ॥

85. Its presiding adept is Pinâkî, and the Kâkini is its goddess. He who always contemplates on this lotus of the heart is eagerly desired by celestial maidens.

ज्ञानञ्चाप्रतिमं तस्य त्रिकालविषयम्भवेत् ।
दूरश्रुतिर्दूरदृष्टिः स्वेच्छया खगतां व्रजेत् ॥ ८६ ॥

86. He gets immeasurable knowledge, knows the past, present and future time; has clairaudience, clairvoyance and can walk in the air, whenever he likes.

सिद्धानां दर्शनञ्चापि योगिनी दर्शनं तथा ।
भवेत्खेचरसिद्धिश्च खेचराणां जयन्तथा ॥ ८७ ॥

87. He sees the adepts, and the goddesses known as Yoginis; obtains the power known as *Khechari*, and conquers all who move in the air.

येा ध्यायति परं नित्यं बाणलिंगं द्वितीयकम् ।
खेचरी भूचरी सिद्धिर्भवेत्तस्य न संशयः ॥ ८८ ॥

88. He who contemplates daily the hidden *Bânalinga*, undoubtedly obtains the psychic powers called Khechari (moving in the air) and Bhuchari (going at will all over the world).

एतद्ध्यानस्य माहात्म्यं कथितुं नैव शक्यते ।
ब्रह्माद्याः सकला देवा गोपयन्ति परन्त्विदम् ॥ ८९ ॥

89. I cannot fully describe the importance of the meditation of this lotus; even the gods Brahmâ etc, keep the method of its contemplation secret.

5. *Vishuddha Chakra.*

अथ विशुद्धचक्रविवरणम् ।
कण्ठस्थानस्थितं पद्मं विशुद्धं नामपञ्चमम् ।
सुहेमाभं स्वरोपेतं षोडशस्वरसंयुतम् ॥
छगलाण्डोऽस्ति सिद्धोत्र शाकिनी चाधिदेवता ॥ ९० ॥

90. This Chakra situated in the throat, is the fifth, and is called the Vishuddha lotus. Its color is like brilliant gold, and it is adorned with sixteen petals and is the seat of the vowel sounds (*i.e.*, its sixteen petals are designated by the sixteen vowels—*a, â, i, î, u, û, ri, rî, lri, lrî, e, ai, o, au, am, ah*. Its presiding adept is called *Chhagalânda*, and its presiding goddess is called *Śâkini*.

ध्यानं करोति येा नित्यं स येागीश्वरपण्डितः ।
किन्त्वस्य येागिनेाऽन्यत्र विशुद्धाख्ये सरोरुहे ॥
चतुर्वेदा विभासन्ते सरहस्या निधेरिव ॥ ९१ ॥

91. He who always contemplates it, is truly the lord of the Yogis, and deserves to be called wise; by the meditation of this Vishuddha lotus, the Yogi at once understands the four *Vedas* with their mysteries.

रहःस्थाने स्थितेा येागी यदा क्रोधवशेा भवेत् ।
तदा समस्तं त्रैलेाक्यं कम्पते नात्र संशयः ॥ ९२ ॥

92. When the Yogi, fixing his mind on this secret spot, feels angry, then undoubtedly all three worlds begin to tremble.

इह स्थाने मनेा यस्य दैवाद्यातिलयं यदा ।
तदा बाह्यं परित्यज्य स्वान्तरे रमते ध्रुवम् ॥ ९३ ॥

93. Even, if by chance, the mind of the Yogi is absorbed in this place, then he becomes unconscious of the external world, and enjoys certainly the inner world.

तस्य न क्षतिमायाति स्वशरीरस्य शक्तितः ।
संवत्सरसहस्रेऽपि वज्रातिकठिनस्य वै ॥ ९४ ॥

94. His body never grows weak, and he retains his full strength for a thousand years, it becomes harder than adamant.

यदा त्यजति तद्ध्यानं योगींद्रोऽवनिमण्डले ।
तदा वर्षसहस्राणि मन्यते तत्क्षणं कृती ॥ ९५ ॥

95. When the Yogi leaves off this contemplation, then to him in this world, thousands of years, appear as so many moments.

6. *Ajña Chakra.*

अथ आज्ञाचक्रविवरणम् ।
आज्ञापद्मं भ्रुवोर्मध्ये हक्षोपेतं द्विपत्रकम् ।
शुक्लाभं तन्महाकालः सिद्धो देव्यत्र हाकिनी ॥ ९६ ॥

96. The two-petalled Chakra, called the Âjña, is situated between the two eye-brows, and has the letters *h*, and *ksh* ; its presiding adept is called *Shuklâ Mahâkâla* (the White Great Time) ; its presiding goddess is called *Hâkinî*.

शरच्चंद्रनिभं तत्राक्षरबीजं विजृंभितम् ।
पुमान् परमहंसोऽयं यज्ज्ञात्वा नावसीदति ॥ ९७ ॥

97. Within that petal, there is the eternal bîja (the syllable ठं ṭhaṃ), brilliant as the autumnal moon. The wise anchorite, by knowing this, is never pulled down.

एतदेव परन्तेजः सर्वतन्त्रेषु मन्त्रिणः ।
चिन्तयित्वा परां सिद्धिं लभते नात्र संशयः ॥ ९८ ॥

98. This is the great light held secret in all the *Tantras*; by contemplating on this, one obtains the highest success, there is no doubt of it.

तुरीयं त्रितयं लिंगं तदाहं मुक्तिदायकः ।
ध्यानमात्रेण योगीन्द्रो मत्समो भवति ध्रुवम् ॥ ९९ ॥

99. I am the giver of salvation, I am the third *linga* in the *turiya* (the state of ecstacy, also the name of the thousand-petalled lotus). By contemplating on this, the Yogi becomes certainly like me.

इडा हि पिंगला ख्याता वरणासीति होच्यते ।
वाराणसी तयोर्मध्ये विश्वनाथोत्र भाषितः ॥ १०० ॥

100. The two vessels called the *Iḍâ* and the *Pingalâ* are the *real Varana* and *Asi*. The space between them is called *Vârânasi* (Benares, the holy city of Śiva). There it is said that the Vishwanâtha (the Lord of the universe) dwells.

एतत्क्षेत्रस्य माहात्म्यमृषिभिस्तत्त्वदर्शिभिः ।
शास्त्रेषु बहुधा प्रोक्तं परं तत्त्वं सुभाषितम् ॥ १०१ ॥

101. The greatness of this holy place has been declared in manifold scriptures by the truth-perceiving sages. Its great secret has been very eloquently dwelt upon by them.

7. *The Thousand-Petalled Lotus.*

सुषुम्णा मेरुणा याता ब्रह्मरन्ध्रं यतोऽस्ति वै ।
ततश्चैषा परावृत्य तदाज्ञापद्मदक्षिणे ॥
वामनासापुटं याति गंगेति परिगीयते ॥ १०२ ॥

102. The *Sushumnâ* goes along the spinal cord up to where the *Brahmarandhra* (the hole of Brahma) is situated. Thence by a certain flexure, it goes to the right side of the Âjña lotus, whence it proceeds to the left nostril, and is called the Ganges.

ब्रह्मरन्ध्रे हि यत्पद्मं सहस्रारं व्यवस्थितम् ।
तत्र कन्देहि या योनिस्तस्यां चन्द्रो व्यवस्थितः ।
त्रिकोणाकारतस्तस्याः सुधा क्षरति सन्ततम् ॥
इडायाममृतं तत्र समं स्रवति चन्द्रमाः ।
अमृतं वहति धारा धारारूपं निरन्तरम् ॥
वामनासापुटं याति गंगेत्युक्ता हि योगिभिः ॥ १०३ ॥

103. The lotus which is situated in the *Brahmarandhra* is called *Sahasrâra* (the thousand-petalled). In the space in its centre, dwells the moon. From that triangular place, elixir is continually exuding. This moon-fluid of immortality unceasingly flows through the *Iḍâ*. The elixir flows in a stream,—a continuous stream. Going to the left nostril, it receives from the Yogis the name of the "Ganges."

आज्ञापङ्कजदक्षांसाद्वामनासापुटंगता ।
उदग्वहेति तत्रेडा वरणा समुदाहृता ॥ १०४ ॥

104. From the right-side portion of the Âjña lotus and going to the left nostril flows the *Iḍâ*. It is here called Varana (the northward-flowing Ganges).

ततो द्वयोर्हि मध्ये तु वाराणसीति चिन्तयेत् ।
तदाकारा पिंगलापि तदाज्ञाकमलान्तरे ॥
दक्षनासापुटे याति प्रोक्तास्माभिरसीति वै ॥ १०५ ॥

105. Let the Yogi contemplate on the space between the two (*Iḍâ and Pingalâ*) as *Vârânasi* (Benares). The *Pingalâ* also comes in the same way from the left side portion of the Âjña lotus, and goes to the right nostril, and has been called by us the *Asi*.

मूलाधारे हि यत्पद्मं चतुष्पत्रं व्यवस्थितम् ।
तत्र मध्येहि या योनिस्तस्यां सूर्यो व्यवस्थितः ॥ १०६ ॥

106. The lotus which is situated in the Mulâdhâr has four petals. In the space between them, dwells the sun.

तत्सूर्यमण्डलद्वाराद्विषं क्षरति सन्ततम् ।
पिंगलायां विषं तत्र समर्पयति तापनः ॥ १०७ ॥

107. From that sphere of the sun, poison exudes continuously. That excessively heating venom flows full through the *Pingalâ.*

विषं तत्र वहन्ती या धारारूपं निरन्तरम् ।
दक्षनासापुटे याति कल्पितेयन्तु पूर्ववत् ॥ १०८ ॥

108. The venom (sun-fluid of mortality) which flows there continuously in a stream goes to the right nostril, as the moon-fluid of immortality goes to the left.

आज्ञापङ्कजवामास्याद्दक्षनासापुटं गता ।
उदग्वहा पिंगलापि पुरासीति प्रकीर्तिता ॥ १०९ ॥

109. Rising from the left-side of the Âjña lotus and going to the right nostril, this northward flowing Pingalâ has been called of yore the Asi.

आज्ञापद्ममिदं प्रोक्तं यत्र देवो महेश्वरः ।
पीठत्रयं ततश्चोर्ध्वं निरुक्तं योगचिन्तकैः ॥
तद्बिन्दुनादशक्त्याख्यं भालपद्मे व्यवस्थितम् ॥ ११० ॥

110. The two-petalled Âjña-lotus has been thus described where dwells the God Maheshwara. The Yogis describe three more sacred stages above this. They are called *Vindu, Nâda* and *Śakti*, and are situated in the lotus of the forehead.

यः करोति सदाध्यानमाज्ञापद्मस्य गोपितम् ।
पूर्वजन्मकृतं कर्म विनश्येदविरोधतः ॥ १११ ॥

111. He who always contemplates on the hidden Âjña lotus, at once destroys all the *karmas* of his past life, without any oppostion.

इह स्थिते यदा योगी ध्यानं कुर्यान्निरन्तरम् ।
तदा करोति प्रतिमां पूजाजपमनर्थवत् ॥ ११२ ॥

112. Remaining in this place, when the Yogi meditates constantly, then to him all forms, worships and prayers appear as worthless.

यक्षराक्षसगन्धर्वा अप्सरोगणकिन्नराः ।
सेवन्ते चरणौ तस्य सर्वे तस्य वशानुगाः ॥ ११३ ॥

113. The Yakshas, Râkshashas, Gandharvas, Apsarâs, and Kinnaras, all serve at his feet. They become obedient to his command.

करोति रसनां योगी प्रविष्टां विपरीतगाम् ।
लम्बिकोर्ध्वेषु गर्तेषु धृत्वा ध्यानं भयापहम् ॥
अस्मिन् स्थाने मनो यस्य क्षणार्धं वर्ततेऽचलम् ।
तस्य सर्वाणि पापानि संक्षयं यान्ति तत्क्षणात् ॥ ११४ ॥

114. By reversing the tongue and placing it in the long hollow of the palate, let the Yogi enter into contemplation, that destroys all fears. All his sins, whose mind remains steady here even for a second,—are at once destroyed.

यानि यानि हि प्रोक्तानि पंचपद्मे फलानि वै ।
तानि सर्वाणि सुतरामेतज्ज्ञानाद्भवन्ति हि ॥ ११५ ॥

115. All the fruits which have been described above as resulting from the contemplation of the other five lotuses, are obtained through the knowledge of this one Âjña lotus alone.

यः करोति सदाभ्यासमाज्ञा पद्मे विचक्षणः ।
वासनाया महाबन्धं तिरस्कृत्य प्रमोदते ॥ ११६ ॥

116. The wise one, who continually practises contemplation of this Âjñalotus, becomes free from the mighty chain of desires, and enjoys happiness.

प्राणप्रयाणसमये तत्पद्मं यः स्मरन्सुधीः ।
त्यजेत्प्राणं स धर्मात्मा परमात्मनि लीयते ॥ ११७ ॥

117. When at the time of death, the Yogi contemplates on this lotus, leaving this life, that holy one is absorbed in the Paramâtmâ.

तिष्ठन् गच्छन् स्वपन् जाग्रत् यो ध्यानं कुरुते नरः ।
पापकर्मविकुर्वाणो नहि मज्जति किल्बिषे ॥ ११८ ॥

118. He who contemplates on this, standing or walking, sleeping or waking, is not touched by sins, even if it were possible for him to do sinful works.

योगी बन्धाद्विनिर्मुक्तः स्वीयया प्रभया स्वयम् ।
द्विदलध्यानमाहात्म्यं कथितुं नैव शक्यते ॥
ब्रह्मादिदेवताश्चैव किञ्चिन्मत्तो विदन्ति ते ॥ ११९ ॥

119. The Yogi becomes free from the chain by his own exertion. The importance of the contemplation of the two-petalled lotus cannot be fully described. Even the gods like Brahmâ, etc., have learnt only a portion of its grandeur from me.

The Thousand-Petalled Lotus.

अत ऊर्ध्वं तालुमूले सहस्रारंसरोरुहम् ।
अस्ति यत्र सुषुम्णाया मूलं सविवरं स्थितम् ॥ १२० ॥

120. Above this, at the base of the palate, is the thousand-petalled lotus, in that part where the hole of that *Sushumnâ* is.

तालुमूले सुषुम्णा सा अधोवक्त्रा प्रवर्तते ।
मूला धारेणयोन्यस्ताः सर्वनाड्यः समाश्रिताः ॥
ता बीजभूतास्तत्त्वस्य ब्रह्ममार्गप्रदायिकाः ॥ १२१ ॥

121. From the base or root of the palate, the *Sushumnâ* extends downwards, till it reaches the *Mulâdhâr* and the perinaeum: all vessels surround it, or are supported by it. These *nâḍis* are the seeds of mystery, or the sources of all principles which constitute a man, and show the road to Brahma (*i.e.* give salvation).

तालुस्थाने च यत्पद्मं सहस्रारं पुराहितम् ।
तत्कन्दे योनिरेकास्ति पश्चिमाभिमुखी मता ॥ १२२ ॥

122. The lotus which is at the root of the palate is called the *Sahasrâr* (the thousand-petalled); in its centre, there is a *Yoni* (seat or force-çentre) which has its face downwards.

तस्या मध्ये सुषुम्णाया मूलं सविवरं स्थितम् ।
ब्रह्मरन्ध्रं तदेवोक्तमामूलाधारपङ्कजम् ॥ १२३ ॥

123. In that is the root of the *Sushumnâ*, together with its hole; this is called the *Brahmarandhra* (the hole of Brahma), extending up to the Mulâdhâr padma.

ततस्तद्रन्ध्रे तच्छक्तिः सुषुम्णा कुण्डली सदा ।
सुषुम्णायां सदा शक्तिश्चित्रा स्यान्मम वल्लभे ॥
तस्यां मम मते कार्या ब्रह्मरन्ध्रादिकल्पना ॥ १२४ ॥

124. In that hole of the *Sushumnâ* there dwells as its inner force the Kunḍalini. In the *Sushumnâ* there is also a constant current of force called *chitrâ*, its actions or modifications should be called, in my opinion as *Brahmarandhra*, etc.

यस्याः स्मरणमात्रेण ब्रह्मज्ञत्वं प्रजायते ।
पापक्षयश्च भवति न भूयः पुरुषो भवेत् ॥ १२५ ॥

125. By simply remembering this, one obtains the knowledge of Brahman, all sins are destroyed, and one is never born again as man.

प्रवेशितं चलाङ्गुष्ठं मुखे स्वस्य निवेशयेत् ।
तेनात्र न वहत्येव देहचारी समीरणः ॥ १२६ ॥

126. Let him thrust the moving thumb into its mouth : by this the air, which flows through the body, is stopped.

तेन संसारचक्रेऽस्मिन् भ्रमतीत्येव सर्वदा ।
तदर्थं ये प्रवर्तन्ते योगी न प्राणधारणे ।
तत एवाखिला नाडी विरुद्धा चाष्टवेष्टनम् ।
इयं कुण्डलिनी शक्ती रन्ध्रं त्यजति नान्यथा ॥ १२७ ॥

127. Owing to this (*vâyu*) man wanders in the circle of the universe ; the Yogis, therefore, do not desire to keep up this circulation ; all the *nâḍis* are bound by eight knots ; only this *kuṇḍalini* can pierce these knots and pass out of the *Brahmarandhra*, and show the way to salvation.

यदा पूर्णासु नाडीषु सन्निरुद्धानिलास्तदा ।
बन्धत्यागेन कुण्डल्या मुखं रन्ध्राद् बहिर्भवेत् ॥ १२८ ॥

128. When the air is confined fully in all the vessels, then the Kuṇḍalini leaves these knots and forces its way out of the Brahmarandhra.

सुषुम्नायां सदैवायं वहेत्प्राणसमीरणः ।
मूलपद्मस्थिता योनिर्वामदक्षिणकोणतः ॥
इडापिंगलयोर्मध्ये सुषुम्ना योनिमध्यगा ॥ १२९ ॥

129. Then the vital air continually flows in the Sushumnâ. On the right and the left side of the Mulâdhâr, are situated the *Iḍâ* and the *Pingalâ*. The Sushumnâ passes through the middle of it.

ब्रह्मरन्ध्रं तु तत्रैव सुषुम्नाधारमण्डले ।
यो जानाति स मुक्तः स्यात्कर्मबन्धाद्विचक्षणः ॥ १३० ॥

130. The hollow of the Sushumnâ in the sphere of the âdhâr is called the Brahmarandhra. The wise one who knows this is emancipated from the chain of karma.

ब्रह्मरन्ध्रमुखे तासां संगमः स्यादसंशयः ।
तस्मिन्स्नाने स्नातकानां मुक्तिः स्यादविरोधतः ॥ १३१ ॥

131. All these three vessels meet certainly at the mouth of the Brahmarandhra ; by bathing at this place one certainly obtains salvation.

The Sacred Triveni (*Prayâg*).

गंगायमुनयोर्मध्ये वहत्येषा सरस्वती ।
तासां तु संगमे स्नात्वा धन्यो याति परां गतिम् ॥ १३२ ॥

132. Between the Ganges and the Jamuna, flows this Saraswati : by bathing at their junction, the fortunate one obtains salvation.

इडा गंगा पुरा प्रोक्ता पिंगला चार्कपुत्रिका ।
मध्या सरस्वती प्रोक्ता तासां संगोऽतिदुर्लभः ॥ १३३ ॥

133. We have said before that the *Iḍâ* is the Ganges and the *Pingalâ* is the daughter of the sun (the Jamuna), in the middle the Sushumnâ is the Saraswati;—the place where all three join is a most inaccessible one.

सितासिते संगमे यो मनसा स्नानमाचरेत् ।
सर्वपापविनिर्मुक्तो याति ब्रह्म सनातनम् ॥ ३४ ॥

134. He who performs mental bathing at the junction of the White (*Iḍâ*) and the Black (*Pingala*) becomes free from all sins, and reaches the eternal Brahma.

त्रिवेण्यां संगमे यो वै पितृकर्म समाचरेत् ।
तारयित्वा पितॄन्सर्वान्स याति परमां गतिम् ॥ १३५ ॥

135. He who performs the funeral rites of his ancestors at the junction of these three rivers (*Triveni*) procures salvation for his aucestors and himself reaches the highest end.

नित्यं नैमित्तिकं काम्यं प्रत्यहं यः समाचरेत् ।
मनसा चिन्तयित्वा तु सोऽक्षयं फलमाप्नुयात् ॥ १३६ ॥

136. He who daily performs the threefold duties (*i.e.*, the regular, occasional and the optional ones) by mentally meditating on this place, receives the unfading reward.

सकृद्यः कुरुते स्नानं स्वर्गे सौख्यं भुनक्ति सः ।
दग्ध्वा पापानशेषान्वै योगी शुद्धमतिः स्वयम् ॥ १३७ ॥

137. He who once bathes at this sacred place enjoys heavenly felicity, his manifold sins are burned, he becomes a pure-minded Yogi.

अपवित्रः पवित्रो वा सर्वावस्थां गतोपि वा ।
स्नानाचरणमात्रेण पूतो भवति नान्यथा ॥ १३८ ॥

138. Whether pure or impure, in whatever state one might be, by performing ablution at this mystic place, he becomes undoubtedly holy.

मृत्युकाले प्लुतं देहं त्रिवेण्याः सलिले यदा ।
विचिन्त्य यस्त्यजेत्प्राणान्स तदा मोक्षमाप्नुयात् ॥ १३९ ॥

139. At the time of death let him bathe himself in the water of this *Triveni* (the Trinity of rivers): he who dies thinking on this, reaches salvation then and there.

नातःपरतरं गुह्यं त्रिषु लोकेषु विद्यते ।
गोप्तव्यं तत्प्रयत्नेन न व्याख्येयं कदाचन ॥ १४० ॥

140. There is no greater secret than this throughout the three worlds. This should be kept secret with great care. It ought never to be revealed.

ब्रह्मरन्ध्रे मनो दत्त्वा क्षणार्धं यदि तिष्ठति ।
सर्वपापविनिर्मुक्तः स याति परमां गतिम् ॥ १४१ ॥

141. If the mind becomes steadily fixed even for half a second at the *Brahmarandhra*, one becomes free from sins and reaches the highest end.

अस्मिँल्लीनं मनो यस्य स योगी मयि लीयते ।
अणिमादिगुणान्भुक्त्वा स्वेच्छया पुरुषोत्तमः ॥ १४२ ॥

142. The holy Yogi whose mind is absorbed in this, is absorbed in me after having enjoyed the powers called *animâ*, *laghimâ* etc.

एतद्रन्ध्रध्यानमात्रेण मर्त्यः संसारे स्यिन्वल्लभो मे भवेत्सः ।
पापाञ्जित्वा मुक्तिमार्गाधिकारी, ज्ञानं दत्त्वा तारयत्यद्भुतं वै ॥ १४३ ॥

143. The man knowing this *Brahmarandhra*, becomes my beloved in this world; conquering sins, he becomes entitled to salvation; by spreading knowledge, he saves thousands of people.

चतुर्मुखादित्रिदशैरगम्यं योगिवल्लभम् ।
प्रयत्नेन सुगोप्यं तद्ब्रह्मरन्ध्रं मयोदितम् ॥ १४४ ॥

144. The Four-faced and gods can hardly obtain this knowledge. it is the most invaluable treasure of the Yogis; this mystery of the *Brahmarandhra* should be kept a great secret.

The Moon of Mystery.

पुरा मयोक्ता या योनिः सहस्रारे सरोरुहे ।
तस्याऽधो वर्तते चन्द्रस्तद्ध्यानं क्रियते बुधैः ॥ १४५ ॥

145. I have said before that there is a force-centre (*yoni*) in the middle of the *Sahasrâra*; below that is the moon; let the wise contemplate this.

यस्य स्मरणमात्रेण योगीन्द्रोऽवनिमण्डले ।
पूज्यो भवति देवानां सिद्धानां सम्मतो भवेत् ॥ १४६ ॥

146. By contemplating on this the Yogi becomes adorable in this world, and is respected by gods and adepts.

शिरःकपालविवरे ध्यायेद्दुग्धमहोदधिम् ।
तत्र स्थित्वा सहस्रारे पद्मे चन्द्रं विचिन्तयेत् ॥ १४७ ॥

147. In the sinus of the forehead let him contemplate on the ocean of milk; from that place let him meditate on the moon, which is in the *Sahasrâra*.

शिरःकपालविवरे द्विरष्टकलया युतः ।
पीयूषभानुहंसाख्यं भावयेत्तं निरंजनम् ।
निरन्तरकृताभ्यासात्त्रिदिने पश्यति ध्रुवम् ।
दृष्टिमात्रेण पापौघं दहत्येव स साधकः ॥ १४८ ॥

148. In the sinus of the forehead there is the nectar-containing moon, having sixteen digits (*kalás*, *i.e.*, full). Let him contemplate on this stainless one. By constant practice, he sees it in three days. By merely seeing it, the practitioner burns all his sins.

अनागतञ्च स्फुरति चित्तशुद्धिर्भवेत्खलु ।
सद्यः कृत्वापि दहति महापातकपञ्चकम् ॥ १४९ ॥

149. The future reveals itself to him, his mind becomes pure; and though he might have committed the five great sins, by a moment's contemplation of this he destroys them.

आनुकूल्यं ग्रहा यान्ति सर्वे नश्यन्त्युपद्रवाः ।
उपसर्गाः शमं यान्ति युद्धे जयमवाप्नुयात् ।
खेचरीभूचरीसिद्धिर्भवेत्क्षीरेन्दुदर्शनात् ।
ध्यानादेवभवे त्सर्वं नात्र कार्या विचारणा ।
सततताभ्यासयोगेन सिद्धो भवति नान्यथा ।
सत्यं सत्यं पुनः सत्यं मम तुल्यो भवेद्ध्रुवम् ।
योगशास्त्रेऽप्यभिरतं योगिनां सिद्धिदायकम् ॥ १५० ॥

150. All the heavenly bodies (planets, etc.,) become auspicious, all dangers are destroyed, all accidents are warded off, success is obtained in war; the *Khechari* and the *Bhuchari* powers are acquired by the seeing of the moon which is in the head. By mere contemplation on it all these results ensue, there is no doubt of it. By constant practice of Yoga one verily becomes an adept. Verily, verily, again most verily, he becomes certainly my equal. The continual study of the science of Yoga, gives success to the Yogis.

Here ends the description of the Ajñapura Chakra.

The Mystic Mount Kailás.

अथ राजयोगकथनम् ।
अत ऊर्ध्वं दिव्यरूपं सहस्रारं सरोरुहम् ।
ब्रह्माण्डाख्यस्य देहस्य बाह्ये तिष्ठति मुक्तिदम् ॥ १५१ ॥

151. Above this (*i.e.*, the lunar sphere) is the brilliant thousand-petalled lotus. It is outside this microcosm of the body, it is the giver of salvation.

कैलासो नाम तस्यैव महेशो यत्र तिष्ठति ।
नकुलाख्योऽविनाशी च क्षयवृद्धिविवर्जितः ॥ १५२ ॥

152. Its name is verily the *Kailâs* mount, where dwells the great Lord (Shiva,) who is called Nakula and is without destruction, and without increase or decrease.

स्थानस्यास्य ज्ञानमात्रेण नृणां, संसारेऽस्मिन्सम्भवो नैव भूयः ।
भूतग्रामं सन्तताभ्यासयोगात्कर्तुं हर्तुं स्याच्च शक्तिः समग्रा ॥ १५३ ॥

153. Men, as soon as they discover this most secret place, become free from re-births in this universe. By the practice of this Yoga he gets the power of creating or destroying the creation, this aggregate of elements.

स्थाने परे हंसनिवासभूते, कैलासनाम्नीह निविष्टचेताः ।
योगी हतव्याधिरधः कृताधिवरायुश्चिरं जीवति मृत्युमुक्तः ॥ १५४ ॥

154. When the mind is steadily fixed at this place, which is the residence of the Great Swan and is called *Kailâs*, then that Yogi, devoid of diseases and subduing all accidents, lives for a great age, free from death.

चित्तवृत्तिर्यदा लीना कुलाख्ये परमेश्वरे ।
तदा समाधिसाम्येन योगी निश्चलतां व्रजेत् ॥ १५५ ॥

155. When the mind of the Yogi is absorbed in the Great God called the Kulâ, then the fullness of the *Samâdhi* is attained, then the Yogi gets steadfastness.

निरन्तरकृते ध्याने जगद्विस्मरणं भवेत् ।
तदा विचित्रसामर्थ्यं योगिनो भवति ध्रुवम् ॥ १५६ ॥

156. By constant meditation one forgets the world, then in sooth the Yogi obtains wonderful power.

तस्माद्गलितपीयूषं पिबेद्योगी निरन्तरम् ।
मृत्योर्मृत्युं विधायाशु कुलं जित्वा सरोरुहे ।
अत्र कुण्डलिनी शक्तिर्लयं याति कुलाभिधा ।
तदा चतुर्विधा सृष्टिर्लीयते परमात्मनि ॥ १५७ ॥

157. Let the Yogi continually drink the nectar which flows out of it; by this he gives law to death, and conquers the *kulâ*. Here the *kulâ kundalini* force is absorbed, after this the quadruple creation is absorbed in the Param Âtman.

The Râja Yoga.

यज्ज्ञात्वा प्राप्य विषयं चित्तवृत्तिर्विलीयते ।
तस्मिन् परिश्रमं योगी करोति निरपेक्षकः ॥ १५८ ॥

158. By this knowledge, the modifications of the mind are suspended, however active they may be: therefore, let the Yogi untiringly and unselfishly try to obtain this knowledge.

चित्तवृत्तियदालीना तस्मिन् योगी भवेद् ध्रुवम् ।
तदा विज्ञायतेऽखण्डज्ञानरूपो निरञ्जनः ॥ १५९ ॥

159. When the modifications of the thinking principle are suspended, then one certainly becomes a Yogi; then is known the Indivisible, holy, pure Gnosis.

ब्रह्माण्डबाह्ये संचिंत्य स्वप्रतीकं यथोदितम् ।
तमावेश्य महच्छून्यं चिन्तयेदविरोधतः ॥ १६० ॥

160. Let him contemplate on his own reflection in the sky as beyond the Cosmic Egg: in the manner previously described. Through that let him think on the Great Void unceasingly.

आद्यन्तमध्यशून्यं तत्कोटिसूर्यसमप्रभम् ।
चन्द्रकोटिप्रतीकाशमभ्यस्य सिद्धिमाप्नुयात् ॥ १६१ ॥

161. The Great Void, whose beginning is void, whose middle is void, whose end is void, has the brilliancy of tens of millions of suns, and the coolness of tens of millions of moons. By contemplating continually on this, one obtains success.

एतद्ध्यानं सदा कुर्यादनालस्यं दिने दिने ।
तस्य स्यात्सकला सिद्धिर्वत्सराान्नात्र संशयः ॥ १६२ ॥

162. Let him practise with energy daily this dhyâna, within a year he will obtain all success undoubtedly.

क्षणार्धं निश्चलं तत्र मनो यस्य भवेद् ध्रुवम् ।
स एव योगी सद्भक्तः सर्वलोकेषु पूजितः ॥ १६३ ॥

163. He whose mind is absorbed in that place even for a second, is certainly a Yogi, and a good devotee, and is reverenced in all worlds.

तस्य कल्मषसंघातस्तत्क्षणादेव नश्यति ॥ १६४ ॥

164. All his stores of sins are at once verily destroyed.

यं दृष्ट्वा न प्रवर्तते मृत्युसंसारवर्त्मनि ।
अभ्यसेत्तं प्रयत्नेन स्वाधिष्ठानेन वर्त्मना ॥ १६५ ॥

165. By seeing it one never returns to the path of this mortal universe; let the Yogi, therefore, practise this with great care by the path of the *Swâdhisthân.*

एतद्ध्यानस्य माहात्म्यं मया वक्तुं न शक्यते ।
यः साधयति जानाति सोऽस्माकमपि सम्मतः ॥ १६६ ॥

166. I cannot describe the grandeur of this contemplation. He who practises, knows. He becomes respected by me.

ध्यानादेव विजानाति विचित्रेक्षणसम्भवम्।
अणिमादिगुणोपेतो भवत्येव न संशयः ॥ १६७ ॥

167. By meditation one at once knows the wonderful effects of this Yoga (*i.e.*, of the contemplation of the void); undoubtedly he attains the psychic powers, called *animâ* and *laghimâ*, etc.

राजयोगो मयाख्यातः सर्वतन्त्रेषु गोपितः।
राजाधिराजयोगोऽयं कथयामि समासतः ॥ १६८ ॥

168. Thus have I described the Râja Yoga, it is kept secret in all the Tantras; now I shall describe to you briefly the Râjâdhirâj Yoga.

The Râjâdhirâj Yoga.

स्वस्तिकञ्चासनं कृत्वा सुमठे जन्तुवर्जिते।
गुरुं संपूज्य यत्नेन ध्यानमेतत्समाचरेत् ॥ १६९ ॥

169. Sitting in the *Swastikâsana*, in a beautiful monastery, free from all men and animals, having paid respects to his Guru, let the Yogi practise this contemplation.

निरालम्बं भवेज्जीवं ज्ञात्वा वेदान्तयुक्तितः।
निरालम्बं मनः कृत्वा न किञ्चिच्चिन्तयेत्सुधीः ॥ १७० ॥

170. Knowing through the arguments of the Vedanta that the Jîva is independent and self-supported, let him make his mind also self-supported; and let him not contemplate anything else.

एतद्ध्यानान्महासिद्धिर्भवत्येव न संशयः।
वृत्तिहीनं मनः कृत्वा पूर्णरूपं स्वयं भवेत् ॥ १७१ ॥

171. Undoubtedly, by this contemplation the highest success (*mahâ-siddhi*) is obtained, by making the mind functionless; he himself becomes perfectly Full.

साधयेत्सततं यो वै स योगी विगतस्पृहः।
अहंनाम न कोऽप्यस्ति सर्वदात्मैव विद्यते ॥ १७२ ॥

172. He who practises this always, is the real passionless Yogi, he never uses the word "I," but always finds himself full of âtman.

को बन्धः कस्य वा मोक्ष एकं पश्येत्सदा हि सः।
एतत्करोति यो नित्यं स मुक्तो नात्र संशयः ॥ १७३ ॥

173. What is bondage, what is emancipation? To him ever all is *one*; undoubtedly, he who practises this always, is the really emancipated.

स एव योगी सद्भक्तः सर्वलोकेषु पूजितः ।
अहमस्मीति यन्मत्वा जीवात्मपरमात्मनोः ।
अहं त्वमेतदुभयं त्यक्त्वाखण्डं विचिन्तयेत् ।
अध्यारोपापवादाभ्यां यत्र सर्वं विलीयते ।
तद्बीजमाश्रयेद्योगी सर्वसंगविवर्जितः ॥ १७४ ॥

174. He is the Yogi, he is the true devotee, he is worshipped in all the worlds, who contemplates the Jivâtmâ and the Pâramatmâ as related to each other as "I" and "Am," who renounces "I" and "thou" and contemplates the indivisible; the Yogi free from all attachment takes shelter of that contemplation in which, through the knowledge of superimposition and negation, all is dissolved.

अपरोक्षं चिदानन्दं पूर्णं त्यक्त्वा भ्रमाकुलाः ।
परोक्षं चापरोक्षं च कृत्वा मूढा भ्रमन्ति वै ॥ १७५ ॥

175. Leaving that Brahma, who is manifest, who is knowledge, who is bliss, and who is absolute consciousness, the deluded wander about, vainly discussing the manifested and the unmanifested.

चराचरमिदं विश्वं परोक्षं यः करोति च ।
अपरोक्षं परं ब्रह्म त्यक्तं तस्मिन् प्रलीयते ॥ १७६ ॥

176. He who meditates on this movable and immovable universe, that is really unmanifest, but abandons the supreme Brahman—directly manifest—is verily absorbed in this universe.

ज्ञानकारणमज्ञानं यथा नोत्पद्यते भृशम् ।
अभ्यासं कुरुते योगी सदा सङ्गविवर्जितम् ॥ १७७ ॥

177. The Yogi, free from all attachment, constantly exerts himself in keeping up this practice that leads to Gnosis, so that there may not be again the up-heaval of Ignorance.

सर्वेन्द्रियाणि संयम्य विषयेभ्यो विचक्षणः ।
विषयेभ्यः सुषुप्त्यैव तिष्ठेत्संगविवर्जितः ॥ १७८ ॥

178. The wise one, by restraining all his senses from their objects, and being free from all company, remains in the midst of these objects, as if in deep sleep, *i.e.*, does not perceive them.

एवमभ्यसतो नित्यं स्वप्रकाशं प्रकाशते ।
श्रोतुं बुद्धिसमर्थार्थं निवर्तन्ते गुरोर्गिरः ।
तदभ्यासवशादेकं स्वतो ज्ञानं प्रवर्तते ॥ १७९ ॥

179. Thus constantly practising the Self-luminous becomes manifest: here end all the teachings of the Guru, (they can help the student no further).

Henceforth he must help himself, they can no more increase his reason or power, henceforth by the mere force of his own practice he must gain the Gnosis.

यतो वाचो निवर्तन्ते अप्राप्य मनसा सह ।
साधनादमलं ज्ञानं स्वयं स्फुरति तद्ध्रुवम् ॥ १८० ॥

180. That Gnosis from which the speech and mind turn back baffled, is only to be obtained through practice; for then this pure Gnosis bursts forth of itself.

हठं विना राजयोगो राजयोगं विना हठः ।
तस्मात्प्रवर्तते योगी हठे सद्गुरुमार्गतः ॥ १८१ ॥

181. The Haṭha Yoga cannot be obtained without the Râja Yoga, nor can the Râja Yoga be attained without the Haṭha Yoga. Therefore, let the Yogi first learn the Haṭha Yoga from the instructions of the wise Guru.

स्थिते देहे जीवति च योगं न श्रियते भृशम् ।
इन्द्रियार्थोपभोगेषु स जीवति न संशयः ॥ १८२ ॥

182. He who, while living in this physical body, does not practise Yoga, is living merely for the sake of sensual enjoyments.

अभ्यासपाकपर्यन्तं मिताशं स्मरणं भवेत्
अन्यथा साधनं धीमान् कर्तुं पारयतीह न ॥ १८३ ॥

183. From the time he begins till the time he gains perfect mastery, let the Yogi eat moderately and abstemiously, otherwise, however clever, he cannot gain success.

अतीवसाधुसंलापोवदेत् संसदिबुद्धिमान् ।
करोति पिण्डरक्षार्थं बह्वालापविवर्जितः ।
त्यज्यते त्यज्यते सङ्गं सर्वथा त्यज्यते भृशम् ।
अन्यथा न लभेन्मुक्तिं सत्यं सत्यं मयोदितम् ॥ १८४ ॥

184. The wise Yogi in an assembly should utter words of highest good, but should not talk much: he eats a little to keep up his physical frame; let him renounce the company of men, let him renounce the company of men, verily, let him renounce all company: otherwise he cannot attain *mukti* (salvation); verily, I tell you the truth.

गुप्त्यैव क्रियतेऽभ्यासः संगं त्यक्त्वा तदन्तरे ।
व्यवहाराय कर्तव्यो बाह्ये संगानुरागतः ।
स्वे स्वे कर्मणि वर्तंते सर्वे ते कर्मसम्भवाः ।
निमित्तमात्रं करणे न दोषोऽस्ति कदाचन ॥ १८५ ॥

185. Let him practise this in secrecy, free from the company of men, in a retired place. For the sake of appearances, he should remain in society, but should not have his heart in it. He should not renounce the duties of his profession, caste or rank; but let him perform these merely, as an instrument of the Lord, without any thought of the event. By thus doing there is no sin.

एवं निश्चित्य सुधिया गृहस्थोपि यदाचरेत् ।
तदा सिद्धिमवाप्नोति नात्र कार्या विचारणा ॥ १८६ ॥

186. Even the house-holder (*grihastha*), by wisely following this method, may obtain success, there is no doubt of it.

पापपुण्यविनिर्मुक्तः परित्यक्ताङ्गसाधकः ।
यो भवेत्स विमुक्तः स्याद् गृहे तिष्ठन्सदा गृही ।
न पापपुण्यैर्लिप्येत योगयुक्तो सदा गृही ।
कुर्वन्नपि तदा पापान्स्वकार्ये लोकसंग्रहे ॥ १८७ ॥

187. Remaining in the midst of the family, always doing the duties of the house-holder, he who is free from merits and demerits, and has restrained his senses, attains salvation. The house-holder practising Yoga is not touched by sins, if to protect mankind he does any sin, he is not polluted by it.

The Mantra ओं ऐं क्लीं स्त्रीं

अधुना संप्रवक्ष्यामि मन्त्रसाधनमुत्तमम् ।
ऐहिकामुष्मिकसुखं येन स्यादविरोधतः ॥ १८८ ॥

188. Now I shall tell you the best of practices, the japa of *mantra*: from this, one gains happiness in this as well in the world beyond this.

यस्मिन्मन्त्रे वरे ज्ञाते योगसिद्धिर्भवेत्खलु ।
योगेन साधकेन्द्रस्य सर्वैश्वर्यसुखप्रदा ॥ १८९ ॥

189. By knowing this highest of the *mantras*, the Yogi certainly attains success (*siddhi*): this gives all power and pleasure to the one-pointed Yogi.

मूलाधारेस्ति यत्पद्मं चतुर्दलसमन्वितम् ।
तन्मध्ये वाग्भवं बीजं विस्फुरन्तं तडित्प्रभम् ॥ १९० ॥

190. In the four-petalled Mulâdhâr lotus is the bîja of speech, brilliant as lightning (*i.e.*, the syllable ऐं *aiṃ*.)

हृदये कामबीजंतु बन्धूककुसुमप्रभम् ।
आज्ञारविन्दे शक्त्याख्यं चन्द्रकोटिसमप्रभम् ॥
बीजत्रयमिदं गोप्यं भुक्तिमुक्तिफलप्रदम् ।
एतन्मन्त्रत्रयं योगी साधयेत्सिद्धिसाधकः ॥ १९१ ॥

191. In the heart is the bîja of love, beautiful as the *bandhuk* flower (क्लीं klim.) In the space between the two eyebrows (*i.e.*, in the Âjña lotus,) is the bîja of Śakti (स्त्रीं strîm), brilliant as tens of millions of moons. These three seeds should be kept secret—they give enjoyment and emancipation. Let the Yogi repeat these three *mantras* and try to attain success.

(*N. B.*—The mystical names of these bîja *mantras* are not given in the text. The whole mantra is Om, aim, klim, strîm.

एतन्मन्त्रं गुरोर्लब्ध्वा न द्रुतं न विलम्बितम् ।
अक्षराक्षरसन्धानं निःसन्दिग्धमना जपेत् ॥ १९२ ॥

192. Let him learn this *mantra* from his Guru, let him repeat it neither too fast nor too slowly, keeping the mind free from all doubts, and understanding the mystic relation between the letters of the *mantra.*

तद्गतश्चैकचित्तश्च शास्त्रोक्तविधिना सुधीः ।
देव्यास्तु पुरतो लक्षं हुत्वा लक्षत्रयं जपेत् ॥ १९३ ॥

193. The wise Yogi, intently fixing his attention on this *mantra*, performing all the duties peculiar to his caste, should perform one hundred thousand *homs* (fire sacrifices,) and then repeat this *mantra* three hundred thousand times in the presence of the Goddess Tripura.

करवीरप्रसूनन्तु गुड़क्षीराज्यसंयुतम् ।
कुण्डे योन्याकृते धीमाञ्जपान्ते जुहुयात्सुधीः ॥ १९४ ॥

194. At the end of this sacred repetition (*japa*), let the wise Yogi again perform *hom*, in a triangular hollow, with sugar, milk, butter and the flower of *karavi* (oleander).

अनुष्ठाने कृते धीमान्पूर्वसेवा कृता भवेत् ।
ततो ददाति कामान्वै देवी त्रिपुरभैरवी ॥ १९५ ॥

195. By this performance of Homa-Japa-Homa, the Goddess Tripura Bhairavi, who has been propitiated by the above *mantra*, becomes pleased, and grants all the desires of the Yogi.

गुरुं सन्तोष्य विधिवल्लब्ध्वा मन्त्रवरोत्तमम् ।
अनेन विधिना युक्तो मन्दभाग्योऽपि सिध्यति ॥ १९६ ॥

196. Having satisfied the Guru and having received this highest of *mantras*, in the proper way, and performing its repetition in the way laid down, with mind concentrated, even the most heavy-burdened with past Karmas attains success.

लक्षमेकं जपेद्यस्तु साधको विजितेन्द्रियः ।
दर्शनात्तस्य क्षुभ्यन्ते योषितो मदनातुराः ॥
पतन्ति साधकस्याग्रे निर्लज्जा भयवर्जिताः ॥ १९७ ॥

197. The Yogi, who having controlled his senses, repeats this *mantra* one hundred thousand times, gains the power of attracting others.

अस्तेन चेद्द्विलक्षेण ये यस्मिन्विषये स्थिताः ।
आगच्छन्ति यथातीर्थं विमुक्तकुलविग्रहाः ॥
ददति तस्य सर्वस्वं तस्यैव च वशे स्थिताः ॥ १९८ ॥

198. By repeating it two lacs of times he can control all persons—they come to him as freely, as women go to a pilgrimage. They give him all that they possess, and remain always under his control.

त्रिभिर्लक्षैस्तथाजप्तैर्मण्डलीकाः समण्डलाः ।
वशमायान्ति ते सर्वे नात्र कार्या विचारणा ॥१९९॥

199. By repeating this *mantra* three *lacs* of times, all the deities presiding over the spheres as well as the spheres, are brought under his dominion.

षड्भिर्लक्षैर्महीपालं सभृत्यबलवाहनम् ॥ २०० ॥

200. By repeating this six *lacs* of times, he becomes the vehicle of power—yea, the protector of the world—surrounded by servants.

लक्षैर्द्वादशभिर्जप्तैर्यक्षरक्षोरगेश्वराः ।
वशमायान्ति ते सर्वे आज्ञां कुर्वन्ति नित्यशः ॥ २०१ ॥

201. By repeating this twelve *lacs* of times, the lords of Yakshas, Râkshas and the *Nâgas* come under his control; all obey his command constantly.

त्रिपञ्चलक्षजप्तैस्तु साधकेन्द्रस्य धीमतः ।
सिद्धविद्याधराश्चैव गन्धर्वाप्सरसांगणाः ॥
वशमायान्ति ते सर्वे नात्र कार्या विचारणा ।
हठाच्छ्रवणविज्ञानं सर्वज्ञत्वं प्रजायते ॥ २०२ ॥

202. By repeating this fifteen *lacs* of times, the Siddhas, the Viddyâdharâs, the Gandharvas, the Apsarâs come under the control of the Yogi. There is no doubt of it. He attains immediately the knowledge of all audition and thus all-knowinghood.

तथाष्टादशभिर्लक्षैर्देहेनानेन साधकः ।
उत्तिष्ठेन्मेदिनीं त्यक्त्वा दिव्यदेहस्तु जायते ॥
भ्रमते स्वेच्छया लोके छिद्रां पश्यति मेदिनीम् ॥ २०३ ॥

203. By repeating this eighteen *lacs* of times, he, in this body, can rise from the ground: he attains verily the luminous body; he goes all over

the universe, wherever he likes; he sees the pores of the earth, *i.e.*, he sees the interspaces and the molecules of this solid earth.

अष्टाविंशतिभिर्लक्षैर्विद्याधरपतिर्भवेत् ।
साधकस्तु भवेद्धीमान्कामरूपो महाबलः ॥
त्रिंशल्लक्षैस्तथाजस्तैर्ब्रह्मविष्णुसमो भवेत् ।
रुद्रत्वं षष्टिभिर्लक्षैरमरत्वमशीतिभिः ॥
कोट्यैकया महायोगी लीयते परमे पदे ।
साधकस्तु भवेद्योगी त्रैलोक्ये सोऽतिदुर्लभः ॥ २०४ ॥

204. By repeating this 28 *lacs* of times, he becomes the lord of the Viddyâdharâs, the wise Yogi becomes *kâma-rûpi* (*i.e.*, can assume whatever form he desires.) By repeating these thirty lacs of times he becomes equal to *Brahmâ* and *Vishnu*. He becomes a Rudra, by sixty *lac* repetitions, by eighty *lac* repetitions he becomes all-enjoyer, by repeating one tens of millions of times, the great Yogi is absorbed in the Param Brahman. Such a practitioner is hardly to be found throughout the three worlds.

त्रिपुरे त्रिपुरन्त्वेकं शिवं परमकारणम् ।
अक्षयं तत्पदं शान्तमप्रमेयमनामयम् ॥
लभतेऽसौ न सन्देहो धीमान्सर्वमभीप्सितम् ॥ २०५ ॥

205. O Goddess! Shiva, the destroyer of Tripura, is the One first and the Highest cause. The wise attains Him, who is unchanging, undecaying, all peace, immeasureable and free from all ills—the Highest Goal.

शिवविद्या महाविद्या गुप्ता चाग्रे महेश्वरी ।
मद्भाषितमिदं शास्त्रं गोपनीयमतो बुधैः ॥ २०६ ॥

206. O great Goddess! this science of Shiva is a great science (*mâhâvidyâ*), it had always been kept secret. Therefore, this science revealed by me, the wise should keep secret.

हठविद्या परं गोप्या योगिना सिद्धिमिच्छता ।
भवेद्वीर्यवती गुप्ता निर्वीर्या च प्रकाशिता ॥ २०७ ॥

207. The Yogi, desirous of success, should keep the Haṭha Yoga as a great secret. It becomes fruitful while kept secret, revealed it loses its power.

य इदं पठते नित्यमाद्योपान्तं विचक्षणः ।
योगसिद्धिर्भवेत्तस्य क्रमेणैव न संशयः ॥
समोक्षं लभते धीमान्य इदं नित्यमर्चयेत् ॥ २०८ ॥

208. The wise one, who reads it daily from beginning to end, undoubtedly, gradually obtains success in Yoga He attains emancipation who honors it daily.

मोक्षार्थिभ्यश्च सर्वेभ्यः साधुभ्यः श्रावयेदपि ।
क्रियायुक्तस्य सिद्धिः स्यादक्रियस्य कथम्भवेत् ॥ २०९ ॥

209. Let this science be recited to all holy men, who desire emancipation. By practice success is obtained, without it how can success follow.

तस्मात्क्रियाविधानेन कर्तव्या योगिपुंगवैः ।
यदृच्छालाभसन्तुष्टः सन्त्यक्तान्तरसंज्ञकः ॥
गृहस्थश्चाप्यनासक्तः स मुक्तो योगसाधनात् ॥ २१० ॥

210. Therefore, the Yogis should perform Yoga according to the rules of practice. He who is contented with what he gets, who restrains his senses, being a house-holder, who is not absorbed in the house-hold duties, certainly attains emancipation by the practice of Yoga.

गृहस्थानां भवेत्सिद्धिरीश्वराणां जपेन वै ।
योगक्रियाभियुक्तानां तस्मात्संयतते गृही ॥ २११ ॥

211. Even the lordly house-holders obtain success by *japa*, if they perform the duties of Yoga properly. Let, therefore, a house-holder also exert in Yoga (his wealth and condition of life are no obstacles in this.)

गेहे स्थित्वा पुत्रदारादिपूर्णः
सङ्गं त्यक्त्वा चान्तरे योगमार्गे ।
सिद्धेश्चिह्नं वीक्ष्य पश्चाद् गृहस्थः
क्रीडेत्सो वै मम्मतं साधयित्वा ॥ २१२ ॥

212. Living in the house amidst wife and children, but being free from attachments to them, practising Yoga in secrecy, a house-holder even finds marks of success (slowly crowning his efforts), and thus following this teaching of mine, he ever lives in blissful happiness.

इति श्रीशिवसंहितायां हरगौरीसंवादे योगशास्त्रे
पंचमः पटलः समाप्तः ॥ ५ ॥ शुभम् ॥